Grammar: A Friendly Approach

Grammar: A Friendly Approach

Second edition

Christine Sinclair

Open University Press

Open University Press
McGraw-Hill Education
McGraw-Hill House
Shoppenhangers Road
Maidenhead
Berkshire
England
SL6 2QL

email: enquiries@openup.co.uk
world wide web: www.openup.co.uk

and Two Penn Plaza, New York, NY 10121-2289, USA

First published 2007
Reprinted 2009
First published in this second edition 2010

A catalogue record of this book is available from the British Library

ISBN-13: 978-0-33-524086-9
ISBN-10: 0-33-524086-0

Library of Congress Cataloging-in-Publication Data
CIP data applied for

Typeset by RefineCatch Limited, Bungay, Suffolk
Printed in the UK by Bell & Bain Ltd., Glasgow

The **McGraw·Hill** Companies

Mixed Sources

Product group from well-managed
forests and other controlled sources
www.fsc.org Cert no. TT-COC-002769
© 1996 Forest Stewardship Council

For my father – Edward Patterson – who taught me about grammar . . . and not sneering.

With special thanks to Jan Smith, Rowena Murray, Marina Orsini-Jones and her students, and the Scottish Effective Learning Advisers.

Contents

List of figures

Introduction to the second edition

When people heard that I'd written a grammar book, they started getting twitchy in my presence. Had they used the wrong word? Was it safe to send me an email? I became uneasy myself; I didn't want to be regarded as an 'expert', called on to make judgements about arcane points of usage. I just wanted to point out that knowledge of how our language works can be very useful to our thinking and writing. That was – and still is – the main purpose of *Grammar: A Friendly Approach*. Parts of speech and sentence structure (see Figures 0.1 and 0.2) should not be puzzling to any graduates who have to write in English.

As I started to use my own book in discussions with students, I became aware that I had some additional things to say. Students are raising new issues about ways of expressing themselves in a rapidly changing climate of ideas and knowledge exchange. Some struggle to find their own voice among many competing ones. 'Do they want my opinion?' is frequently heard from students in the humanities, while many science students question the need to be doing any writing at all. While such problems have been around for some time, technology is having an additional impact.

Knowing how language works might help us to understand how it changes when it goes to different places – for example, to phones, websites or social networking. Technology brings not only new language practices but also new ways of monitoring those practices, such as grammar checkers and software that 'detects' plagiarism. The latter is such a major current issue for universities all over the world that it seemed important to build it into the account of our changing language practices.

Having a soap opera in my book has allowed me to track the shifting contexts for debates about grammar, language and punctuation. While my main characters – Barbara, Abel and Kim – have been trying to take control of their own problems with academic language and sentence construction, experts in computational linguistics have developed software that can detect, correct and even grade our students' language practices. For some students I've met since I planned the first edition of the book, a new fear has been emerging: technology might mercilessly expose and condemn their unwitting errors and unintended plagiarism.

We don't want students to lose their ability to say anything for fear of wrongdoing. Whether a sneer comes from a user of Standard English or from a software program, it does not provide a suitable framework for bringing out what you are trying to say. I hope that such a framework can be found in *Grammar: A Friendly Approach*.

Part of speech	Description	Examples
Verb	Word showing action	be, do, have, learn, teach
Noun	Name of person, place, thing, idea	mother, Paris, table, existentialism
Pronoun	Word that stands for a noun	I, him, it, this, whose, someone, nobody
Adjective	Word that describes – usually goes with a noun or a pronoun	attractive, dusty, gentle, red
Adverb	Word that modifies a verb or adjective, or other adverb (often ends in -ly)	fully, gracefully, usually, very
Articles	These are special types of adjective, showing whether the noun is indefinite or definite.	
	Indefinite	a, an
	Definite	the
Preposition	Word that indicates a relationship	for, through, to, up
Conjunction	Joining word	and, but, or (joining expressions of equal importance – co-ordinating)
		because, though, when (joining something less to something more important – subordinating)
Interjection	Word expressing emotion which is unrelated to the rest of the sentence (usually not appropriate for academic writing)	alas, ha-ha, wowee

Figure 0.1   Parts of speech

This page shows some of the issues from the book in a simplified visual form, especially those in Chapters 6, 7 and 9. Sentences can contain other elements, such as complements and phrases. See the Glossary for the meanings of the words used in the illustration.

1 Simple sentence

You might also see this called a principal clause, a main clause or an independent clause. There is often an object, but not always.

2 Compound sentence

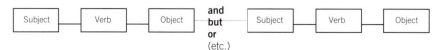

3 Complex sentence

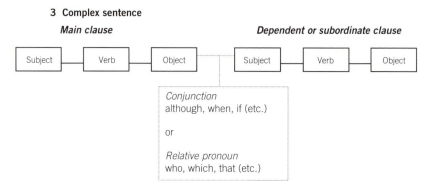

Figure 0.2   Building blocks of sentences

1

Introduction

1.1 A soap opera in a grammar book • 1.2 Questions about grammar • 1.3 How the book is structured • 1.4 How to annoy teachers and professors • 1.5 What students worry about • 1.6 Comments on questions • 1.7 Conclusion: general advice about grammar and language

This is a good time for grammar and punctuation. Lynne Truss's runaway success with *Eats, Shoots and Leaves* (2003) shows that people welcome high standards in language use and want to ensure that we can all communicate clearly and effectively. After years when many UK schools did not teach grammar explicitly, the subject has started to reappear. A number of writers are now showing us that it does not have to be a dry, dull subject.

This book is for all university or college students who have been told that they 'need to do something about grammar' or are worried that their grammar is not up to scratch. It is also for anyone who is interested in grammar and how it works, including school students. Some school teachers and college or university lecturers feel anxious about grammar too: you might be surprised at how many.

The term 'grammar' has a broad meaning here, including language use and punctuation as well as sentence structure. The book is not as comprehensive as some other grammar books and websites, and there are suggestions for further reading in the Bibliography. Its purpose is different from those books.

1.1 A soap opera in a grammar book

I have worked in three different universities – ancient, modern, and a former polytechnic. In all three, I have seen many students who have problems with grammar and use of language. Although there are some excellent books on grammar and punctuation, the students who come to see me often tell me that they don't know where to start with them. There are too many technical terms to learn and rules that seem to be broken all the time. The books seem far removed from the day-to-day problems of writing at university.

Grammar and punctuation do not just exist as sets of arbitrary rules to annoy students who are writing essays; they help us to make sense of the world. Most of us are able to use excellent grammatical structures without too much thought, especially when we're speaking. There are just a few typical muddles when people write things down and this book attempts to cover the most common difficulties. We are writing things down a great deal more now-adays, if texts, emails and other communications using technology are taken into account.

I wanted to write the book because I thought that students need advice set in the kind of context that actually happens. I have tried to bring the issues alive by making them happen to three students: Abel, Barbara and Kim. These characters are based on real students that I meet – especially their problems and their responses to them. To give the context a bit of a story, I have added some details about the students' lives that I would not normally hear about. This is a grammar book with a soap opera in it.

1.2 Questions about grammar

1 What is grammar?
2 Why might grammar be important?
3 What are the main things that go wrong with grammar, language and punctuation?

These are not easy questions! There are some suggestions in Section 1.6.

1.3 How the book is structured

Each chapter is devoted to a particular issue related to language, grammar or punctuation. It starts with a story where the students face the issue and help each other to resolve it. There are then some questions to encourage you to think where you are with this topic, and some advice which might involve more bits of the story. The stories build up over the book, but you can also read them as individual scenes.

The language used in the book itself is informal – I am not writing in an academic style. However, there are also some technical terms. A lot of grammar is about naming types of words and the relationships between them. It can be useful for you to know about the technical terms, in case anyone uses them with you, for example in giving feedback on an essay. At the end of each chapter, I have suggested the terms that you could look up in more comprehensive grammar books or on the World Wide Web, where there are many useful sites.

There is a Glossary at the end of the book where you can look up specific topics and, if appropriate, it tells you which chapters you can find them in. So, for example, if you have been having problems with *inverted commas*, the Glossary draws your attention to Chapter 10's Figure 10.3, which looks at the functions of different punctuation marks. It also highlights Chapter 13. If a word appears in the Glossary, it is (usually) in italics the first time it is used in this book.

The book can be read in several ways, depending on your needs. You can read it right through and see the stories and the grammatical points build up. The more complex grammatical points tend to be later in the book. Alternatively, if you want to get information about a particular point, you might use the Contents list, the Glossary or the Index to find out where that point is likely to be.

Each chapter concludes with a summary of the main advice given in the chapter. If you are in a real hurry, you might just want to go straight to the conclusion of the chapter.

1.4 How to annoy teachers and professors

I asked a group of academics from different subject areas what really annoyed them about students' grammar and language use. They said they really hated it when students:

1 Use apostrophes wrongly
2 Confuse common words; for example, there/their
3 Make spelling errors
4 Use informal language
5 Write sentences without verbs
6 Make every sentence a paragraph
7 Don't use paragraphs
8 Write long convoluted sentences

9 Try to write too pompously
10 Use run-on sentences and comma splices.

All of these topics, and a lot more, are considered in this book. Here's a quick reference to where to find the information.

1 The *apostrophe* has a chapter of its own – Chapter 11.
2 Chapter 2 looks at easily confused words, especially in Section 2.4.
3 Section 2.5 has some general advice about spelling.
4 You'll find some comments on informal language in Chapters 2 and 3.
5 Chapters 4 and 5 look at *verbs*; Chapter 5, 6 and 7 deal with sentences.
6 Section 6.5 looks at the relationship between sentences and paragraphs.
7 If you don't know what a paragraph is, you'll find out in Chapter 7.
8 Chapters 7 and 9 should help you avoid convoluted sentences.
9 Chapter 2 has warnings about pompous language.
10 Section 7.3 deals with *comma splices*; Chapter 10 also considers *commas*.

1.5 What students worry about

The experiences of three students highlight the grammatical issues in the book. These students went to an informal essay-writing session held at their university soon after Christmas and discovered that they had something in common: they were all getting pulled up for their grammar but didn't know what they could do about it. Here is some background information about them.

> **Barbara** is 18 and in her first year, studying philosophy, English and media studies. She is enjoying university life and being away from home for the first time. In the first semester, she spent more time thinking about her emotional life than her essay writing and was upset to get some low grades. She had split up with her boyfriend at home just before she arrived. During Freshers Week, she met a guy called Mark, and went out with him a few times but she hasn't heard from him for six weeks, despite trying to contact him through texts and Facebook. Mark just seems to have disappeared. She is trying not to let this put her off her studies and has started the second semester determined to improve her grades.
>
> **Abel** is a second year student, studying science – mainly physics and biology. He had a few years out before he came to university; he is 25. He shares a flat with Gus, who is doing the same course, but Abel is starting to regret this as Gus is always asking to borrow food, beer and money. This semester he is taking an

elective on the philosophy of science, which he is finding strangely intriguing, and he is starting to question his choice of subjects and what he wants to do with his degree. He is wondering about becoming a teacher, an idea that would have been totally alien to him a few years ago. He feels that if he doesn't improve his language skills, he is going to limit the options open to him.

Kim is in her final year, hoping to graduate with a good degree in mechanical engineering. In her first couple of years she was irritated by comments about her writing – 'I'm not at University to do English!' However, she now recognizes that engineers have to be able to express themselves clearly too, and as she is thinking about doing further study (possibly a PhD), she needs to do something about her difficulties with writing. She has particular problems with punctuation, but she doesn't understand why people make such a fuss about it. She is just coming up for 21 and planning a big party to celebrate. She lives in a large flat with five other students, so there will be plenty of room.

We'll also meet some of their other friends and relatives and find out a bit more about their personalities during each chapter. Here's an extract from the conversation they have after the essay-writing class. It's pouring with rain when they come out and they run to the café for shelter and coffee. They start to talk about *syntax, synonyms* and the use of a *thesaurus*. All of these words are defined in the Glossary.

Abel:	I keep getting told that my syntax is poor. That would be OK if I knew what it meant!
Kim:	I get that one as well. I thought a syntax error was something to do with computing but apparently it can just mean your grammar's not good.
Barbara:	I looked it up, 'cause I got it as well. It does mean something to do with grammar and sentences – the structure of a sentence. And in computing it's the rules for combining bits of a programming language. So it's similar.
Abel:	Where did you look it up – have you got quite a good dictionary?
Barbara:	Yes – my parents gave me one at Christmas and I was like, great – what do I want that for? But now I'm glad they did; I'm using it loads. I got a thesaurus too.
Abel:	What does that do?
Barbara:	Well, you look it up if you want to find words that are grouped together, or synonyms, you know – have the same meaning.
Kim:	I've got a scientific dictionary – it's quite good. But it doesn't help me with punctuation. Someone gave me a book about that, but I don't understand it. I need something on those inverted comma thingies.

Abel: Is that the same as quotation marks? I've been told I should be using them but I'm not quite sure how. I just bought a grammar book, but I don't really like it. I started to read it and fell asleep.

Barbara: It's good to find other people with the same problems. I've been a bit embarrassed to talk about it. Some of the lecturers seem to put you down if your grammar's not right – you know, they're a bit sneering. I was wondering if there'd be any grammar classes, but you don't like to ask.

Abel: Well, I've just learned a whole load talking to you two – about dictionaries, syntax, synonyms . . . any other 'syns' you want to tell me about? Listen, do you fancy meeting here again another day – I'll bring my grammar book – and we can talk about essays and stuff.

Barbara's very keen on this idea. Kim isn't so sure (Abel's comment on 'syns' has put her off) but they do all arrange to meet a couple of days later and read each others' assignments that have to be handed in over the next week. They all agree that the basic rule is 'no sneering'.

1.6 Comments on questions

1.6.1 What is grammar?

If you look up 'grammar' in a good dictionary (making sure that you spell it with an ar and not an er), you'll probably find at least two types of definition. One type is concerned with grammar as a study of the way we use language; the other type emphasizes correct use and following a set of rules. This book makes reference to both, but points out that 'correct' use can sometimes be contested or controversial. You might find the word *inflection* in the definitions: this refers to the way words change to show their function and how they relate to each other. So, for example, grammar is concerned with why we have all the different endings we can see in words such as play, plays, playing, played, player, players, playful and playfully. It is also concerned with relationships between words: we play in the street, we play the violin, we watch a play, play can help our learning, we play up, we play down, we play around.

1.6.2 Why might grammar be important?

Knowing about grammar will help us to use the correct version of the word for our intended purpose. We mostly do this automatically, however, whether we know about grammar or not. If other people cannot understand what we are saying or think that we have not expressed ourselves clearly, then it may be because there is a grammatical error. People make judgements about others on the basis of the grammar they use; whether this is fair or right, it definitely happens and it is important that you know about it.

1.6.3 What are the main things that go wrong with grammar, language and punctuation?

I read many students' essays and find that the same problems keep coming up. Often the things that go wrong relate to sentence structure. Sentences may be incomplete, or alternatively too long and complicated. There may be confusion about who or what the sentence is about – its *subject*. Perhaps it is hard to see what this subject is doing, has done or will be doing. There can be errors in the words themselves – the wrong spelling, ending or usage. There can also be errors in the way the words relate to each other. Punctuation is supposed to guide us to avoid confusion; often it is used in ways that contribute to the confusion.

1.7 Conclusion: general advice about grammar and language

- It's not your fault if you were not taught grammar at school. It is important to try to get it right now, though.
- The same grammatical errors keep coming up in students' essays. It is useful to know what these are so that you can take steps to avoid them. This book attempts to consider the most common mistakes.
- It's a good idea to have a dictionary that is appropriate for the subjects you are studying. A thesaurus can be useful too, but should be used with care (as you'll see in Chapter 2).
- You can learn a lot from talking to other students. You can also give each other reassurance.

1.7.1 Technical terms relating to this chapter

For further information, look up these words in the Glossary, other grammar books or the World Wide Web.

Inflection
Subject
Synonym
Syntax
Thesaurus

2

Bad language

When you become a university student, you have to learn how to speak and write like the experts in your subject do. It can take students a while to realize this; some feel, for instance, that it is phoney to try to write as a sociologist or a chemical engineer when you're just starting. Some students will try to imitate the style and the attempt doesn't quite work. There seems to be a tension between the writing that you are used to and the writing that you have to do when you're an expert in the subject. It is natural and normal to experience this tension and to have to find your way through it.

Our story illustrates some of the dangers of trying to put fancy words into an essay. Abel has just bought himself a thesaurus and thinks that it is going to solve some of his problems.

2.1 Trying to be posh

Abel is waiting impatiently in the café for the others. He's been fired up with the writing he has been doing on paradigm shifts in science and can't wait to show the others what he has done. When Barbara arrives, he gives her his draft (see Figure 2.1 overleaf) and watches her reaction. She doesn't seem as excited as he is by the subject and in fact looks puzzled.

Barbara: I don't think this is going to work. I don't understand a word of this. Maybe it's because it's about science.

Abel: But it's the philosophy of science. You're doing philosophy too.

Barbara: Well, what does this mean? 'Kuhn further condemns Popper's claim that when a paradigm is falsified it is dishevelled.' Like, what's a 'dishevelled paradigm'?

Abel: Let's see? Oh that's something I got from a book but I changed some of the words. I was looking for another word for 'abandoned' and that sounded quite a good one. Found it in a thesaurus. Maybe it's not quite right though.

Barbara: It's not right – have you got the book there?

Abel hands Barbara *The Ascent of Science* by Brian Silver. He's marked page 105 where he's used large chunks of two paragraphs about Kuhn and Popper.

Barbara: Abel – you've just copied this and changed the odd word. And it doesn't make sense. And this other bit's your own and you're just putting in fancy words for the sake of it.

Kim arrives with an engineering report under her arm.

Kim: Oh, you're hard at it already. Just got myself a thesaurus – they're great.

Barbara: Well, don't do what Abel's just done – he's used it to turn a good piece of writing into crap.

Abel: Wait a minute – no sneering, remember.

Barbara: Well, OK, but you really can't just use a thesaurus like that.

See what you think of Abel's attempt to use a thesaurus. Below is the original passage, followed by Abel's rendering of it. As you read his version of Brian Silver's original, think about how a lecturer might read it. How much sense would it make?

2.1.1 Original writing

Kuhn further rejects Popper's claim that when a paradigm is falsified it is abandoned. According to Kuhn, abandonment of an old paradigm occurs only when a new one is available. In other words, Popper says that when the raft is uninhabitable we jump into the sea, while Kuhn says we jump only when another raft is available.

Popper, in reply, concedes that much science is not carried out with the object of falsifying theories, and he sees such science as second-class. He insists that science as a whole jumps forward by the process of falsification.

(Silver 1998: 105)

2.1.2 Abel's version with additional comment

Kuhn further condemns Popper's claim that when a paradigm is falsified it is dishevelled. The occurrence of an old paradigm tergiversation depends on the availability of a novel one. In other words, Popper retorts that when the the raft is uninhabitable we jump into the sea, while Kuhn stresses the availability of a further raft.

Popper, in reply, is lenient about science that does not have falsification but regards it as second class. He is obstinate that science as a hole jumps forward by the process of falsification.

This postulation of differences illustrate the intransigencies of the two writers and the difficulties of the determination of the shifting of a paradigm. It is the author's opinion that falisfication is not a nescessity but it is something that should be essayed by scientists in there deliberations.

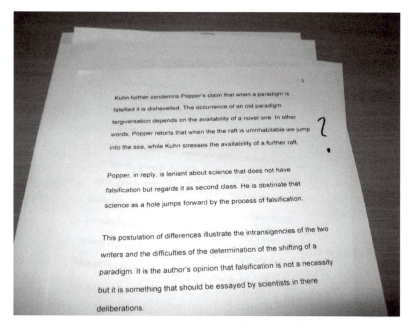

Figure 2.1   An essay that's hard to understand

2.2 Questions about language

1 What errors in language use would you pick out in Abel's writing?
2 Who is the author referred to in the final sentence?
3 Is Barbara right to say that you shouldn't use a thesaurus in this way?
4 How does Brian Silver's piece use the idea of rafts? Should Abel be using it the same way?

The following sections consider typical language errors, including some of the ones in Abel's writing. There are suggested answers to those four questions in Section 2.11. There are also alternative versions of what Abel is trying to say there.

2.3 Idioms: how words are usually used

Some of the examples I am using are ones I have actually seen. A student I saw replaced the word 'abandoned' with 'dishevelled' and I had to explain to her that the only time such a substitution would be appropriate would be when talking about someone's hair or clothes. It was not idiomatic for her to write about a system of government being dishevelled.

By 'idiomatic', I mean 'the way we usually say it'. *Idiom* refers to the distinctive use of language that does not relate particularly to the dictionary meaning of the words used (for example, think about the expression 'kick the bucket'). As with the example of 'abandoned', idiomatic use usually relates to which words can be appropriately used together. Use of correct idiom is often a problem for international students, because English has some very strange expressions. Idiom can also vary in different areas of the UK and US and it can change over time. Academic subjects have their own idioms and it can take some time to get used to them.

If you are unfamiliar with the idiomatic use of a word, then you may cause confusion when you use it as a replacement.

2.4 Easily confused words

One of the most common errors students make is to confuse 'their', 'there' and 'they're'. You may have noticed that Abel had used the wrong one in his last sentence. It is easily done, especially if you are the sort of writer who hears words in your head before you write them down. Like Abel, I often confuse these words if I am writing quickly, but have trained myself to make a mental check that I am using the correct one. It helps to think that the word 'here' is often present in easily confused words that refer to place:

Here	in this place	Hear	use the ear
There	in that place	They're	short for 'they are'
Where	in which place	Were	past *tense* of are

There are many easily confused words. It is not always so easy to find ways of distinguishing them. In Figure 2.2, I have made some suggestions where I can.

These are errors I have particularly noticed when I have looked at students' essays. You can find longer lists of these words in some other books, for example Burt (2004). (See the Bibliography at the end of the book for details.)

Notice that Abel also used 'hole' instead of 'whole' even when he was copying from someone else's writing. If he had checked this carefully, he would probably have recognized that it was wrong; to a lecturer, however, the misspelling just looks illiterate rather than poor checking.

2.5 Going through a bad spell

'. . . falisfication is not a nescessity . . .'

When someone is reading your essay, they will not necessarily be able to tell the difference between typing errors and poor spelling. In either case, the essay may become hard to read. One problem with both kinds of error is that you know what you intended to write and you 'read' what you think is there. That is why it is worth leaving your writing for a couple of days and coming back with a reader's perspective, rather than the writer's. I know how unrealistic this advice can be, but if you can build in checking time it could make a huge difference to your grade.

If you know you are likely to have difficulties with particular words, it is worth checking them in a dictionary and writing down a list correctly spelled. Here is a list of words I frequently see misspelled: this is the correct version.

beautiful	grammar
business	necessary
definite	psychology
desperate	separate
government	writing

The word ...	which means ...	is not ...	which means ...
affect	act upon or influence (verb) Less commonly, it means emotion (noun)	effect	the result of an action (noun) Less commonly, it means to bring about a result (verb)
cite	name (verb)	site	position (noun or verb)
compliment	praise	complement	complete/completion
its	belonging to it	it's	it is Tip: never use 'it's' in academic writing.
practise	work at or carry out (verb) (in UK English)	practice	action or performance (noun) Similarly advise – advice license – licence
principle	origin or rule (noun)	principal	main (adjective) head of a university or college (noun)
stationary	not moving (adjective)	stationery	paper, pens etc. (noun) items that a stationer sells
there	in that place	their	belonging to them
where	in which place	were	past tense of 'are'
whose	a word that indicates belonging, always followed by a noun – 'Whose book is that?'	who's	who is or who has
your	a word that indicates belonging – 'It is your book'	you're	you are Tip: don't use abbreviations. Don't use 'you' anyway.

Figure 2.2 Some easily confused words

2.6 Singulars and plurals

'This postulation of differences illustrate the intransigencies of the two writers . . .'

Apart from being rather pompous, this extract from Abel's essay demonstrates a very common language error – a plural verb (illustrate) is used when a singular was needed. It is the postulation that illustrates the intransigencies. Alternatively (and more readably) Abel could have written:

These differences illustrate . . .

This point relates to how a sentence is put together – using a subject and a verb. There is more on this in Chapter 6.

Singular subject: *This postulation* of differences illustrates . . .
Plural subject: *These differences* illustrate . . .

2.7 Formal doesn't have to mean pompous

When you are at university, you are expected to write formally. Some broad rules for this are:

- **Don't use *abbreviations* such as 'don't'!**
  You'll notice that I'm not attempting to write formally in this book.
- **Avoid slang words and clichés.**
  Clichés are hackneyed or overused expressions such as 'in this day and age', 'the writing on the wall', 'part and parcel'.
- **Avoid words or expressions with emotional or extreme overtones.**
  If you feel that you should use an exclamation mark, then the expression is probably inappropriate.

There is a big difference, though, between avoiding slang and using pompous expressions. In his excitement with the riches of the thesaurus, Abel came across the word 'tergiversate' which means 'to turn one's back; to desert, change sides; to shuffle, shift, use evasions' (*Chambers Dictionary*, 2003). While this might seem appropriate for writing about paradigm shifts, there is a good chance that it would not be idiomatic use. Abel has never seen the word in context so he does not know. The lecturer would probably have to look the word up. The main effect is likely to be a comic one or an irritation, depending on the personality and mood of the lecturer. Abel is unlikely to impress the lecturer with this word.

2.8 What are you trying to say?

One of the problems in writing about language is that we like to tell you what you can't do, but that doesn't help you to decide what words you are able to use.

Abel is understandably upset at Barbara's apparent sneering – breaking the new friends' main rule – which doesn't help him at all to work out what he could be saying. A simple question from Kim saves the day:

What exactly is it that you're trying to say?

Here is Abel's reply:

Well, a paradigm shift is when the whole way of thinking about something changes – like when people realized that the earth goes round the sun instead of the sun going round the earth. That meant that everything had to be rethought. But it wasn't a sudden thing – Copernicus suggested it, then Galileo took it up later and had real problems with the Church because of it. Popper says that when a scientific explanation has been shown to be false, that's when we abandon it. He thinks it's important that we keep trying to falsify scientific thinking, because that's how we advance. But Kuhn's argument is that we need another framework to replace it – you don't get rid of one explanation until you have another one.

I think they're both right: you should try to look for counter-examples or other ways of falsifying the way we think. But you might not find them. As well as trying to show that something's false, it's also useful to look for other ways of saying things. So I don't think it's necessary to prove things false – you don't have to do it – but it's useful to try. The main point of my essay is that we have to be careful that we don't become trapped by our existing ways of looking at things. If everyone just proves what they know already, then science never moves on.

Like many students, Abel finds that he can say it but he can't write it. As soon as he starts to write his own opinion, he gets caught up in whether or not he's entitled to do so. Should he call himself 'the author', for instance?

2.9 The author, one or I?

'It is the author's opinion that . . .'

In some academic writing, the use of 'I' (known as the first *person*) is not acceptable. You should be aware that this is changing and not all lecturers think the same way about it. It is probably worth asking about it, if there is any doubt.

People use a lot of different ways to get round using 'I'. Repeated use of 'the author' can be very tedious, though it can be useful at the start of a piece of writing; for example:

This report was written to record the findings from the author's placement at *x* during the summer of [date].

Another substitution – perhaps less common nowadays – is 'one'. In some subjects it can be a useful way to refer to people in general, for example:

When one observes other people's actions, one must be wary of ascribing intentions that may not be there.

'One' is sometimes used when comedians are trying to parody 'posh' speakers. It can sound rather affected, especially if it is used very frequently. 'It is one's opinion that . . .' would have sounded affected in Abel's essay.

It is not essential to replace 'I' with 'the author' or 'one' – and it does often sound very awkward if you do this. In Abel's case, he could have avoided it altogether. He has found value in both positions he is discussing. He can say this, without having to use 'in my opinion'. For example, he can say that falsification may not be necessary, and can give a reason or some evidence for that claim.

There is more on the debate about the use of 'I' in Chapter 8, Section 8.6.

2.10 It's, like, a figure of speech

Abel suddenly realizes that he understands more about Kuhn and Popper than he has thought and that the answer is not just to cobble together bits from books. The conversation below shows how using another author's *metaphor* or *simile* might be evidence of *plagiarism*.

Abel: Kim – you're great. I'm going to ask myself that whenever I'm stuck. 'What exactly is it that you're trying to say?' Do you do that yourself?

Kim: Yeah – I've always found that useful. Then I have to take out all the stuff like 'I' and 'me' and make it sound neutral. Engineers hate you to use 'I'.

Abel: So do scientists. Well, I think they do. Those who aren't jumping into the sea!

Barbara: Yeah, that's what was so weird about your essay. Why did you need to say stuff about rafts?

Kim: Is that a metaphor or the other thingie? When something's like something.

Abel: Yeah, the raft stuff is a metaphor – I did know that. When you say something is something else. When it's like something it's a simile. So if scientific progress is a raft, then it's a metaphor. If it's like a raft, it's a simile.

Barbara: Can't see the difference.

Abel: How about 'life is a bowl of cherries' – that's a metaphor. Though weird.

Kim: And the movie – *Forest Gump.* 'Life is like a box of chocolates.' Simile.

Barbara: Like chocolates – mmm – now you're talking. Do we need to know this though?

Kim: If you're going to use someone else's metaphor, it's probably a giveaway that you've copied.

Abel: Point taken.

Kim: I know about it. I done it myself once. Got a warning about plagiarism.

Barbara: I done it? Don't you mean 'I did it'?

Abel: No sneering, Barbara. Remember?

Barbara: Not sneering – just pointing out.

Kim: Whatever.

2.11 Comments on questions

2.11.1 What errors in language use would you pick out in Abel's writing?

- The main error he has made is that he has plagiarized someone else's writing. Changing the odd word is not enough.
- In particular, his word substitution is inappropriate. The following words are not idiomatic for their context: condemns, dishevelled, tergiversation, retorts, lenient, obstinate.
- He has accidentally repeated a word (the).
- He has misspelled two words that sound like others: hole for whole and there for their.
- He has misspelled or mistyped 'falsification' and 'necessity'.

2.11.2 Who is the author referred to in the final sentence?

When he uses 'the author's opinion', it is a little confusing. He could be referring to Popper. He might even be referring to Silver, though as he doesn't reference him, there is no way of knowing that. A little thought shows he is referring to himself. But it trips the reader up to have to work this out.

2.11.3 Is Barbara right to say that you shouldn't use a thesaurus in this way?

It is certainly a dangerous practice. This would count as plagiarism in many people's eyes. Sometimes it is necessary to *paraphrase* someone else's writing: that is, to write their point in your own words. It is not a good idea to do this by substituting words, though. If you want to use a thesaurus to find an alternative word, make sure you see examples of that word in context somewhere so that you can be sure that your idiom is correct.

2.11.4 How does Brian Silver's piece use the idea of rafts? Should Abel be using it the same way?

The rafts have been used as a metaphor to illustrate Silver's point. If Abel uses the same metaphor without acknowledgement, it is likely to draw attention to his plagiarism. Metaphors can stand out, especially if they do not fit a student's own style of writing. This metaphor is a particularly useful one, however, as it highlights the idea of a 'container' or 'framework' to support our perspective on the world. The second example below shows how to acknowledge someone else's metaphor. Chapter 13 looks more at plagiarism and how to avoid it.

2.11.5 Alternative ways of writing the section of Abel's essay

1 The work of two writers, Popper and Kuhn, illustrates different ways of explaining scientific advances (Silver 1998). While Popper argues that scientists abandon a principle when it has been shown to be false, Kuhn believes that they do not abandon it until there is another to replace it. Kuhn's work on paradigm shifts suggests that scientists are bound by the paradigms of their own time and place. Although these views are apparently opposing, they both offer some insights into scientific history. Falsification may not be necessary for scientific progress because alternative explanations of the world have arisen without it. It may still be useful, though, to consider both Popper's encouragement to demonstrate that our principles are not false and Kuhn's concerns about the difficulties of seeing beyond our current paradigm.

2 Silver (1998: 105) uses the metaphor of a raft to illustrate the difference between the views of Popper and Kuhn. The raft is the scientific framework, or paradigm. For Popper, the raft becomes uninhabitable – or the scientific framework has been falsified – and scientists have to jump into the sea. For Kuhn, scientists will not abandon the raft unless there is another one. This metaphor usefully highlights two questions: do scientists have to have a paradigm, and do they have to falsify it before they get a new one?

   Scientific progress might happen without overturning a previous paradigm. The arguments of both scientists show, however, that it may be necessary to question our existing way of looking at things.

2.12 Conclusion: advice about word choice

- Become familiar with words that are easily confused and train yourself to spot them.
- Avoid the extremes of slang and pompous writing.
- Think about what you are trying to say, rather than trying to drag an essay from books.
- Don't use an alternative word from a thesaurus or dictionary unless you are familiar with its idiomatic use.
- Learn how to spell the frequently used words in your own subject area.
- You'll get into the way of writing in your subject's style as you grow more familiar with its idioms. If you read a lot, it will help your writing.
- If you are borrowing a metaphor or other figure of speech from another writer, then you should acknowledge this.

2.12.1 Technical terms relating to this chapter

For further information, look up these words in the Glossary, other grammar books or the World Wide Web.

Idiom
Metaphor
Paraphrase
Plagiarism
Simile

The web can be useful for finding meanings of strange idioms. Try googling

Idiom "kick the bucket"

and you'll find various sites that offer an explanation. You can do this with any other expression in double *quotation marks*. (See also Chapter 13.)

3

Standard practice

3.1 Why can't I use my own language? • 3.2 Questions about 'correct' English • 3.3 Standard English: do we need it? • 3.4 Examples of uses that are not standard • 3.5 Spoken and written English • 3.6 Academic English • 3.7 Comments on questions • 3.8 Conclusion: advice about dialects and Standard English*

3.1 Why can't I use my own language?

> *Kim:* What's wrong with 'I done' anyway? Everyone says that.
>
> The students are finding it difficult to give each other constructive advice. They don't know each other well enough yet to feel totally relaxed about teasing, and criticism of what people say can sometimes be taken for 'sneering' even when it's not meant that way. The argument later shows the problems.
>
> *Barbara:* It's just wrong. It's ignorant and illiterate. My mum and dad went over it and over it when I was a kid. If ever I said, 'I've went' or 'I been' they corrected me every time. So I just know it's wrong. 'I done' was another one.
> *Abel:* So when is it right to say 'done'? Is it when you say 'have' before it? So it should be: I have done, I have gone, I have written . . . Or I did, I went, I wrote.
> *Kim:* Barbara, I listen to the football on BBC radio nearly every Saturday. Just last week, they were talking about my team. The manager said, 'The team done better over the first three games of the season'. I remember it clearly.

Barbara: They're just plain wrong. Illiterate. That's footballers for you.

Abel: And what happens with 'of' instead of 'have'?

Barbara: What do you mean 'of'?

Abel: I know it wouldn't be 'I could of did' but would it be 'I could of done'?

Barbara: It shouldn't be 'of' at all, Abel. That's just pure nonsense. It's 'have'. I could have done. Why would you say 'of'? It doesn't make sense.

Kim: I think it must have changed, Barbara. If it's on the radio, it must be OK.

Barbara: No it's not. I have a lot of problems with grammar but I do know this one. It was footballers my dad used to complain about when they came on TV. He said they were illiterate and got paid too much money. He kept saying that I had to get this right or I'd not get into uni.

Kim: Well, that's a load of rubbish then, 'cause I'm here and I get it wrong. Sounds like snobbery and sneering to me.

Abel: Me too. I think it might be old-fashioned. And round here, most people say a mix of 'I done' or 'I have done'. Everyone understands you so why does it matter?

Barbara: 'Course it matters. You've got to have standards. And the educated way is 'I have done'. I'm going to keep saying it and saying it until you've got it into your thick heads.

Kim: Oh shut up, Barbara; you're being a snob. And go and get us another coffee.

Barbara: [*Storms off and shouts over her shoulder*] I did it yesterday. I've done enough for today. I could have done without all this.

3.2 Questions about 'correct' English

1 'I done it' is a way of speaking in some parts of the UK, but not others. Is it used in your area? Can you suggest any similar examples for the area you live in?

2 Should we accept local usages of words in colleges and universities rather than insisting on 'correct' English?

3 Do you know the 'correct' forms of past versions of bring, do, go, see, write? What about the past of the verb 'to be'?

4 Why am I writing 'correct' in quotation marks?

5 Why is 'I could of done' not correct?

There are comments on these questions in Section 3.7.

3.3 Standard English: do we need it?

Standard English refers to 'the form of English taught in schools, etc., and used, esp. in formal situations, by the majority of educated English-speakers' (*Chambers Dictionary*, 2003).

Many of the writers who comment on Standard English point out that it is just one *dialect* of English. (For a definition of 'dialect', see the Glossary, and for examples of writers who talk about language and power, see the Bibliography.) Standard English is the dominant dialect and the one used by the most powerful people in the UK. If you want to be acknowledged as a 'correct' speaker by educated English speakers, you need to be able to use the correct versions of words, such as *past participles* of verbs – the bits that are causing Kim so much difficulty. We'll be looking at verbs in more detail in Chapter 5.

If Standard English is just the dialect that is most successful, and is associated with power, then there is a political aspect to its use. Some people might make a case for saying that another dialect would be more appropriate. As Kim points out, other dialects are also heard on radio and television. So does this mean that we no longer need to bother?

Like Barbara, I grew up with parents who immediately corrected any use of English that was not standard, except when I was using it for particular effect – perhaps a joke. They also commented on 'bad' English used by popular entertainers. This does mean that I hardly ever make these mistakes myself, so I am protected from the judgement that I am 'uneducated' because of the way I speak.

I don't always take such a strong line myself, however. My main concern is that people are able to make themselves understood and I recognize that the language is constantly changing. Even so, if people do make judgements about students because of the verbs they use – and I know that they do because they have told me so – then I firmly believe that those students have a right to know about it. They have a right to decide whether or not they want to use the dominant dialect that gives the impression that they are educated speakers.

3.4 Examples of uses that are not standard

In the introduction, the idea of 'inflection' was introduced in the answer to Question 1. This term refers to the way words change. We add -s to show that *nouns* are plural – books, plays. We also might add -s to show a verb in the third person – The traffic warden books the driver. Kim plays the saxophone. We add -ed to show that something happened in the past: Barbara walked away. The inflection of some words is different in different dialects, especially when there is a verb that is irregular, unlike play, or walk.

Standard English	Examples of variations
I am	I be, I'm are, I is, I are, I bin
you did well	you done good
she does	she do, her does, shoo does,
he does not / doesn't	he don't
he is not / isn't	he aint
it was	it were
we are	we'm, us are
we were	we was
you are	yous are
they are	them are, they's, them's
they have	they han

There are many more examples of variation in English; perhaps you can think of some in your own region.

As well as grammar, you can hear different dialects in how words are pronounced and also in local vocabulary. One interesting example is children's truce terms, of which there were many in the UK, including barley, fainites, keys, nicks, pax, scrogs, trucie. As a child in Aberdeen, I said 'barleys' and crossed my fingers; children where I live now sometimes say 'keys' and give a thumbs up if they want to be out of the game for a bit. Now, though, they are increasingly saying 'timeout' and making a T sign as happens in the US. Barbara wishes she had done that instead of storming off.

3.5 Spoken and written English

Barbara returns with three coffees and a sheepish look.

Barbara: Sorry about the timeout there. I didn't mean to be sneery.

Abel: No, I found it useful actually. You're right about 'could of done' – of isn't a verb. It's how we say it, and how we hear it, but we shouldn't write it.

Kim: And you've helped me realize something I overheard my tutor say on the phone when he didn't know I was outside the door. He was like, 'We can't let her do the presentation to the industrial sponsors because her grammar's so awful'. I want to do that presentation –

	but was he talking about me? Because I say 'I done' instead of 'I did' or 'I have done'. I hope not.
Abel:	So sometimes how you say it matters as well as how you write it.
Kim:	I hate it when people make judgements about you. And I don't want to sound like the Queen when I do a presentation. I could write it all out beforehand, but I'd rather speak naturally. Written language is different from spoken.
Abel:	I can't get it right in writing either. That's why I used the thesaurus. The way other people write things seems to be the only way to do it – I know I'm going to get it wrong if I try myself. It just doesn't sound right. I know I'm in danger of plagiarizing but I can't find the words. Yous are going to have to help me. Sorry, wrong again – I mean you.
Barbara:	Abel – we'll all help each other. And I promise not to sneer; you don't have to worry about saying 'yous'. But don't put it in an essay! Kim, I think you should go and see your tutor and have it out with him.

Kim is right to say that spoken and written English are not the same: her presentation is likely to sound stilted if she writes it all out and then reads it. Some professional speakers can do this, though, as they have a good sense of what will work in speech. Spoken English has more flow and more action; tone of voice can be used to get some of the meaning across. The use of text, email, blogging and tweeting is encouraging more of this flow in written English in general, but many of the new conventions (abbreviations, slang, emoticons etc.) are still inappropriate for academic writing. Written language, however, uses a wider range of words than spoken.

Academics seem to be in two camps about written and spoken language: some complain that students write the way they speak; others say that students write things that they would never say. While academic writing is not really the same as a spoken *genre*, it can be a good idea to test writing for how it sounds by reading it aloud. Abel seems to be having a real problem with what his writing 'sounds' like and is in danger of just copying the writers he admires, which could get him into a lot of trouble. He needs to find a way of writing good *academic English* in his own words.

3.6 Academic English

If you google "academic English" you are likely to find various sites for international students. But even if English is your mother tongue, academic English is not (it isn't anyone's). It refers to ways of writing that have become genres

– for example, the essay, the scientific report, the dissertation. Students are expected to follow conventions for pieces of writing, including:

- Standardized beginnings and endings: e.g. statement of aim and how this is going to be achieved; conclusion showing how it has been achieved
- Neutral language and tone – unbiased and without exaggeration
- Appropriate referencing of other writers
- Using vocabulary appropriate to the academic subject and clarifying any technical terms.

It is difficult to write what is 'appropriate' when you are still learning about this. The best way to learn is to read other writers in your subject. You'll probably find these in journal articles and books more than on websites and Wikipedia. But rather than copy out word for word what authors have written, ask yourself how their writing works – how they are following the conventions listed above.

3.7 Comments on questions

3.7.1 'I done it' is a way of speaking in some parts of the UK, but not others. Is it used in your area? Can you suggest any similar examples for the area you live in?

This usage is quite common in Glasgow where I live – I've had several students say, 'I done quite well in my last essay.' Or, 'I've went over it several times.' In some parts of the UK, though, this would never be said. It is not Standard English and some lecturers will mark you down for using it. All parts of the UK will have similar examples.

3.7.2 Should we accept local usages of words in colleges and universities rather than insisting on 'correct' English?

This is quite a sensitive issue and you'll probably already be aware that I am sympathetic to people who have not been brought up with Standard English as their main dialect.

It is probably appropriate, however, for institutions to encourage certain standards of writing for several reasons:

- Students do not come just from the local area but from other parts of the UK and from other countries too.
- Consistency in language use helps to ensure accuracy and shared meaning.
- The outside world expects certain standards of language use in graduates.

- You may create a poor impression of yourself if you don't use the Standard English terms.

The key issue in all these reasons is that we use language to communicate.

3.7.3 Do you know the 'correct' forms of past versions of bring, do, go, see, write? What about the past of the verb 'to be'?

There are several ways you might have answered this, depending on whether you used the simple past or one with another word such as 'have' or 'has'.

Bring	I brought	I have brought
Do	I did	I have done
Go	I went	I have gone
See	I saw	I have seen
Write	I wrote	I have written
Be	I was	I have been

3.7.4 Why am I writing 'correct' in quotation marks?

The use of *scare quotes* draws attention to my view that being correct is not a simple case of absolute right or wrong; it relates to what the powerful people have decided should be right and wrong and this changes over time. Note that it is not advisable to use too many scare quotes in a piece of academic writing.

3.7.5 Why is 'I could of done' not correct?

The word 'done' is a part of a verb – the past participle. A *participle* needs at least one other verb to complete it: here 'could have' completes it. The word 'of' is not a verb and so it can't fulfil this function. This common error arises because we hear 'of' when we are saying 'have'.

3.8 Conclusion: advice about dialects and Standard English

- While Standard English is just a powerful dialect rather than an absolute correct form that lasts for ever, it pays to know how and when to use it. Your use of past participles, such as 'written' and 'done', can still single you out as someone who has a good education or not.
- At university, you are expected to write in academic English, using particular genres. Some of these may be specific to your own subject area. The best

way to find out what these are is to read journals and books in your subject area. Some students get information from Wikipedia and news websites such as the BBC; these can be useful starting points for information, but will not be sufficient to expose you to academic forms of writing.

- While the emphasis here is on writing, grammatical errors in spoken English can be problematic for some students, especially those who are expected to make presentations.

3.8.1 Technical terms relating to this chapter

For further information, look up these words in the Glossary, other grammar books or the World Wide Web.

Academic English
Dialect
Genre
Past participle (see also Chapter 5)
Scare quotes
Standard English

4

Who or what is the subject?

> The agent in a sentence – i.e. whoever or whatever is 'in charge' of the verb.
>
> (Palmer 2003: 183)

A sentence needs both a subject and a verb (see Figure 4.1). We look at verbs in Chapter 5 before looking at how sentences work (or don't) in Chapters 6 and 7. In this chapter, we find out how being a subject of a sentence relates to doing things or having things done to you. Subjects can be people, things or ideas. The subject is usually the topic of a sentence; the action of the sentence happens in relation to the subject. Subjects and verbs also appear in groups of words that might not be a complete sentence – *clauses*.

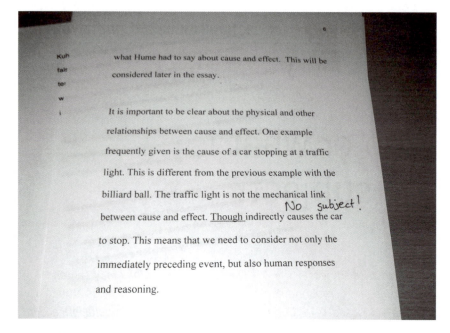

Figure 4.1   A sentence needs a subject

4.1 A favourite subject – 'I'

Barbara is furious when her lecturer writes 'No subject!' in the margin of her essay. She thinks that he means that she hasn't followed the topic. She bumps into Kim and persuades her to have a look at the comment.

Barbara: When I think of the time I spent making sure I understood the question! Of course there's a subject here: the subject's cause and effect.

Kim: No, he doesn't mean the subject of the essay – he's only underlined one sentence. I think you can talk about the subject of a sentence. Where's your dictionary? Look up 'subject' and see if there's anything with 'gram' with the definition. That means it's about grammar.

[Barbara has started to carry her dictionary around with her – though her shoulder hurts because it is so heavy!]

Barbara:	Oh yes – here we go. [*Reads*] 'That part of a sentence or clause denoting the person or thing about which something is said (*gram*).'
Kim:	So what should it be? For the bit he's underlined, you've just written, 'Though indirectly causes the car to stop.' What do you mean? What causes the car to stop?
Barbara:	It's in the sentence before – it's a traffic light. I don't want to keep repeating myself.
Kim:	You still need something to do the causing, even if it's just 'it'. Perhaps this belongs to the previous sentence anyway, because 'though' creates a link. So it should be, 'The traffic light is not the mechanical link between cause and effect, though it indirectly causes the car to stop.' Then the subject of 'is' is 'traffic light' and the subject of 'causes' is 'it'.
Barbara:	D'you know, I think I'd have noticed that if I had read it over. I was late finishing it. It doesn't sound right, does it? 'Though indirectly causes the car to stop.' If I'd spent time checking it, I'd have wondered what that meant.
Kim:	I've starting reading stuff aloud now. It's amazing what you pick up. And I know I've picked up that kind of problem before, but I didn't know it was called the subject of the sentence.
Barbara:	So the subject is what does the action. IT causes the car to stop. BARBARA causes men to behave badly. Like that Mark guy last semester. BARBARA chooses terrible men. What happens with, 'BARBARA is chosen by terrible men'? Am I still the subject?
Kim:	That's a good example. Someone has to do the choosing or be chosen. So Barbara is the subject of the sentence in both cases.
Barbara:	Why don't they teach you that at school? I like being a subject.
Kim:	I've noticed!

4.2 Questions about subjects of sentences

1 Look at a paragraph in a book (e.g. the first paragraph of this chapter). Can you identify the main subject of each sentence in that paragraph?
2 Are there ever sentences without subjects?
3 Can there be more than one subject in a sentence?

There are comments on these question in Section 4.6.

4.3 Simple and compound subjects

The subject is likely to be a noun or *pronoun*. It might also be a *phrase* containing a noun or pronoun. The main subject of a sentence is also likely to come near the beginning of the sentence.

Every sentence (almost – we look briefly at exceptions later) should have a subject and a complete verb. This may be all that the sentence has:

Subject	*Verb*
Barbara	works.
I	have finished.
Ideas	will change.

These are rather short sentences and too many of them together would make the writing jerky and stilted. The main point is that if there is not a verb and a subject for that verb, then it is probably not a sentence. There are some exceptions. For example, 'Please shut the gate.' would be regarded as a sentence, though the subject (you) is not explicit. The exceptions are unusual, however, and it is useful for you to keep reminding yourself that you need a verb and someone or something in charge of it.

There is more detail about what a sentence is in Chapter 6. To help us to build up to that, we need to think some more about subjects and, especially, what can go wrong with them.

The first point to notice is that the subject and the verb should match – or agree, as the grammar books say.

> I work.
> Barbara works.
> He works.
> They work.

Sentences can contain more than one subject; in fact, it is easy to combine the sentences above using a *compound subject*.

> Barbara and I work.
> Barbara and he work.

Then the verb has to be a plural one because the subject is plural.

4.4 When subjects move around

When the sentences are short like those we've just considered, it is unlikely that you will get the *agreement* wrong. But look at the following examples.

> *Barbara*, despite spending a lot of time thinking about Mark, *works* extensively in the early mornings.
> *I* – the author of this book about grammar – *work* at a Scottish university.

In cases like this, the verb becomes separated from the subject. This is because an extra group of words has been added as further description for the subject. (Notice how commas or *dashes* separate off this aside; we return to this in Chapter 10.) The danger here is that in the separation, the writer forgets what the subject is and puts the wrong ending in for the verb. There is also a danger if the subject and verb are too far apart that the reader forgets who or what the sentence is about. Both of the sample sentences above run this risk.

Note that if you removed 'I' from the second example, you would need to change the verb. The subject then becomes 'The author' rather than 'I'.

> *The author* of this book about grammar *works* at a Scottish university.

Sometimes, there is an expression in front of the subject.

> As we are both more alert in the mornings, *Barbara*, who is a fictional character, *and I*, her author, *work* in similar ways.

Here the verb has to be a plural one to take account of the two subjects.

The verb 'to be', as so often happens, has some interesting features. Consider the following expressions.

> I was tired.
> Barbara is a fictional character.

The words after the verb are known as the *complement*, because they complete the verb. The sentence could meaningfully (though not elegantly) be reversed – 'Tired was I'. This is not the case with many verbs which have more of a sense of action (rather than just being): try reversing 'The dog ate the bone', for example. In that case, the meaning changes and, indeed, becomes impossible.

Other expressions that are common with the verb 'to be' are:

> It is . . .
> There is . . .

> There are . . .
> Are there . . .?

These constructions allow for subjects to be in a different place in the sentence, either for emphasis or for effect. In the following expression, the *adverb* 'there' doesn't really have any meaning of its own, but it allows an impersonal way of introducing 'a price' which is effectively the subject of the sentence.

> There is a price to pay for expecting so much from students.

In the case of Jane Austen's famous opening sentence in *Pride and Prejudice*, the pronoun 'it' is the subject, but it serves to highlight the complement 'a truth':

> It is a truth universally acknowledged, that a single man in possession of a good fortune, must be in want of a wife.

If you are interested in finding out more about complements, Palmer (2003) has some useful points. Here I am just introducing the idea so that you are not worried about using such expressions as 'it is' or 'there are'.

4.5 Subject closed

> Barbara and Kim have spent more time thinking about subjects than they intended. Barbara has decided that she's been getting too worked up about grammar.
>
> *Barbara:* There's less to this than meets the eye. So really, all I had to do was make sure there was something or someone that the sentence was about.
> *Kim:* Looks like it.
> *Barbara:* There's a theme coming out here. What am I trying to say? What's going on? Who or what's doing it? Who or what's having it done to them? And why aren't the interesting answers to that question happening to me?
> *Kim:* Your day will come. Perhaps you'll meet someone at my party. Then you can change the subject.

4.6 Comments on questions

4.6.1 Look at a paragraph in a book (e.g. the first paragraph of this chapter). Can you identify the main subject of each sentence in that paragraph?

The main subject of each sentence from the first paragraph of this chapter is in italics. You'll see that the penultimate sentence has two main subjects; it is really two sentences joined with a *semicolon*.

> *A sentence* needs both a subject and a verb (see Figure 4.1). *We* look at verbs in Chapter 5 before looking at how sentences work (or don't) in Chapters 6 and 7. In this chapter, *we* find out how being a subject of a sentence relates to doing things or having things done to you. *Subjects* can be people, things or ideas. *The subject* is usually the topic of a sentence; *the action* of the sentence happens in relation to the subject. *Subjects and verbs* also appear in groups of words that might not be a complete sentence – clauses.

4.6.2 Are there ever sentences without subjects?

It is probably a useful rule of thumb to say that a subject is an essential part of a sentence. However, examples can be found of apparently subjectless sentences – often with implicit subjects as in instructions. 'Shut the door.' is a sentence and the subject is 'you'. 'It is snowing.' is a sentence, but what does it mean to say 'it' is the subject? It certainly does not help if we see a subject as being a topic of a sentence, which is why it is useful to think about grammar and punctuation as well as content for sentences. The main point is that if you are reading over your own writing and it sounds odd, it is always worth checking whether your sentence has a subject or not.

4.6.3 Can there be more than one subject in a sentence?

Subjects can be compound, meaning that there is more than one. There are also separate subjects in clauses that are not the main clause in the sentence (we have not yet looked at this, so don't worry if you did not realize it). Finally, as in the last sentence of the first paragraph of this chapter, sometimes sentences are joined together with a word like 'and' or a semicolon. These sentences will have two main clauses and therefore two subjects.

4.7 Conclusion: advice about sentences and subjects

If something you've written doesn't sound right, ask yourself the following questions:

- Does this sentence have at least one subject?
- Is it clear which subject goes with which verb?
- Are the subject and verb so far apart that their connection is lost?
- Do the subject and verb agree (are they both either singular or plural)?

4.7.1 Technical terms relating to this chapter

For further information, look up these words in the Glossary, other grammar books or the World Wide Web.

Agreement
Complement
Compound subject
Subject

5

Where's the action?
The verb

*5.1 Doing, being and happening • 5.2 Questions about verbs •
5.3 Mangling and dangling participles • 5.4 Getting tense with verbs •
5.5 My past, present and future • 5.6 Facts and possibilities •
5.7 Comments on questions • 5.8 Conclusion: advice about verbs*

5.1 Doing, being and happening

If you recognize the verb in a sentence, you are able to see what is going on. You can tell what the subject is up to, or what state it is in, or what is happening to it. Our students are struggling with this! It doesn't help when you have to look up definitions for your definitions; they need to understand *transitive* and *intransitive*.

Barbara and Kim pass an almost empty classroom, where Abel has his laptop open and his head in his hands.

Barbara: What are you doing, Abel?
Abel: You said the other day that I might be plagiarizing. I'm just check-ing an online dictionary for a definition of 'plagiarize'. I think I know what it means but I started to worry. It says it's a verb, but then it's got two versions, transitive and intransitive. Why does it have to be so complicated?
Kim: *[Reading over Abel's shoulder]* 'transitive verb: to steal and pass off

	(the ideas of words of another) as one's own . . .'. Where's this from, Abel?
Abel:	Merriam-Webster dictionary.
Barbara:	So a synonym for 'plagiarize' is 'steal and pass off as one's own'. Is that one verb, two verbs or what?
Kim:	Yeah – 'pass' and 'pass off' must be different verbs I'd think. So 'steal' is a verb and 'pass off' is a verb.
Barbara:	And the stuff in brackets is what you're passing off. That's an American dictionary, Abel – let's see what mine says. It's much the same: *[reading from Chambers Dictionary]* 'To steal from (the writings and ideas of another)'. I've just noticed in italics vt and vi – I wonder if that's verb transitive and verb intransitive. But we'll have to look that up too.
Abel:	'intransitive verb: to commit literary theft.' Oh dear.
Barbara:	*[Reading from Chambers Dictionary]* 'intransitive . . . representing action confined to the subject of the verb, ie having no object'. So when it's intransitive, when you plagiarize, it's all about you. You steal. You are a plagiarizer.
Abel:	Don't.
Barbara:	And when it's transitive, there's an object – there's something you plagiarize. I suppose steal is just the same: you steal my book; you steal – end of story.
Kim:	Barbara, you're not saying this in a very positive way.
Barbara:	I'm just trying to get at the verbs. It's not personal. But it's not just action: you are a plagiarizer – are is about being. 'Plagiarism happens' – plagiarism is the subject but there's not really any action in happening. But I think 'happens' is a verb too.
Kim:	The definition says 'to steal' – so where's the subject there?
Barbara:	I think we're going to have to find out a bit more about how verbs work. Perhaps we should use a different one; this one's upsetting Abel too much.

Here is how the Merriam-Webster website reference should be *cited*.

plagiarize (2009). In *Merriam-Webster Online Dictionary*. Retrieved June 21, 2009, from http: www.merriam-webster.com/dictionary/plagiarize

5.2 Questions about verbs

1 Try to find the verbs in the following passage from *Zen and the Art of Motorcycle Maintenance*. Note that the verb might not just be a single word; it may be a phrase.

> He was systematic, but to say he thought and acted like a machine would be to misunderstand the nature of his thought. It was not like pistons and wheels and gears all moving at once, massive and co-ordinated. The image of a laser beam comes to mind instead; a single pencil of light of such terrific energy in such extreme concentration it can be shot at the moon and its reflection [can be] seen back on earth. Phaedrus did not try to use his brilliance for general illumination. He sought one specific distant target and aimed for it and hit it. And that was all. General illumination of that target he hit now seems to be left for me.
>
> (Pirsig 1974: 80)

2 'Write' is a verb: 'writing' and 'written' are what are known as participles. Why do these two words not count as complete verbs?
3 Should you write an essay using the past tense or the present tense?
4 Is 'google' a verb?

There are comments on these questions in Section 5.7.

5.3 Mangling and dangling participles

> work – verb
> working – *present participle*
> worked – past participle

Participles are parts of verbs. Present participles always end in -ing and past ones often end in -ed. They are used in various forms relating to the past, present and future. We have already come across past participles in Chapter 3, when we looked at some non-standard ones that might vary with local use (written, done, been etc.). Other things that go wrong with participles are that they are misspelled or *misrelated* (especially when they are used as *adjectives*).

5.3.1 Present participles

Though the ending is always -ing, people sometimes get confused with present participles because a letter is doubled or an e is removed. A very small number just don't quite follow the rules. The following lists might help if you're stuck.

Add -ing	Double a letter	Lose an e	Odd
being	cutting	advising	dying
bringing	getting	coming	dyeing
doing	hopping	filing	panicking
falling	nodding	hoping	
filling	sinning	judging	
going	stirring	noticing	
playing	stopping	practising	
seeing		shining	
singeing		writing	
singing			
studying			
working			

Barbara wasn't too happy to get a comment on an essay that said *'dangling participle!'*, especially after she'd made such a fuss about getting past participles right. It's usually the present participle that gets dangled, when it's being used to modify another part of the sentence. Here's Barbara's example:

Being a man of considerable means, Jane Austen wanted Mr Darcy to be the focus of attention.

When she talked to Kim about it, Kim thought she could see what the lecturer meant. 'It looks as if you're saying that Jane Austen was a man of considerable means.'

Barbara didn't think it did, but when she looked up 'dangling participle' in some books, she realized that if you have a word such as 'being', it should relate to the main part of the sentence appropriately. It did look as though she was saying that Jane Austen was a man!

Here are some alternatives.

Being a man of considerable means, Mr Darcy was used by Jane Austen as a focus of attention.

Jane Austen wanted Mr Darcy, being a man of considerable means, to be the focus of attention.

The problem with starting a sentence with a present participle is that the reader immediately wonders who or what this expression relates to. If it is *misrelated* (or dangling) then it trips the reader up. It can lead to unconscious humour, for example:

Reading about Africa, the lion seems to be the main predator.
(Which books are the lions reading?)

Sipping a cold beer, my golden retriever was at my feet and my book was
open at my favourite poem.

(Did the dog and book share the beer?)

5.3.2 Past participles

The following lists might help you to remember how to spell the past participles
and also when to use them. Past participles always need another verb – such as
have, has, had, is, was, will be . . . We'll come back to this in Section 5.4.

Add -ed	Add -d	Double a letter	Odd/irregular
filled	advised	hopped	been
played	died	nodded	brought
worked	dyed	sinned	come
	filed	stirred	done
You may need to	hoped	stopped	gone
change a y to i first	judged		got
	practised		fallen
emptied	singed		led
studied			panicked
			read
			seen
			shone
			sung
			written

Sometimes people confuse the past and present participles. Students
occasionally send me an email along the lines of, 'I am writting for an
appointment'. This is incorrect: the double t makes the i sound different (as
in 'written'), but the present participle has a long i and the word should be
'writing'.

5.4 Getting tense with verbs

Abel has arrived first at the café as Barbara has stopped to pick up her essay.
He's skimming through a chapter of a book that he needs for his tutorial. He is
soon interrupted when Barbara does arrive; she's obviously in a bad mood. She
flings her essay on the table. Abel looks at the cover. The mark's not too bad,
but there is a single comment on it – *Tenses!* Her tutor clearly doesn't like to
waste too much ink on feedback.

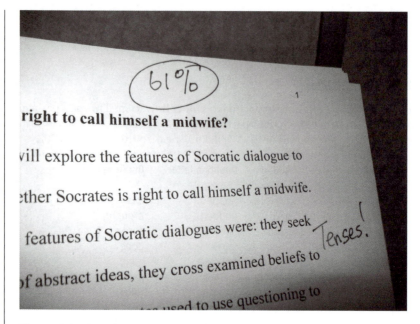

Figure 5.1 A verb needs a tense

Barbara: What's that supposed to mean? Is it good, or bad – or what?
Abel: 'Tenses' means past and present and future. Maybe you've used the wrong one. Give me a look.
Barbara: Well, I don't know what she's talking about. See if you can work it out and I'll get myself a drink.

Abel looks at the essay, takes out a pencil and lightly underlines each verb in the first paragraph. Barbara comes back with a cappuccino.

Barbara: Hey – what are you doing?
Abel: I'm finding it confusing too, so I thought I'd underline the verbs and see if I could work it out. Look, this bit's future, this is in the present – and I'm not sure what this is supposed to be!
Barbara: Well, perhaps it should all be in the past. Plato has been dead for quite some time!
Abel: Yes, but his writing is still here. And I think sometimes you see that and sometimes you don't. And that's when you get things mixed up.
Barbara: I suppose if I'm talking about his ideas, they still sort of exist because they're still being discussed. But when Plato's writing about what Socrates did, shouldn't that be in the past? And it's kind of hard to separate the ideas from what Socrates did. So

should I say 'Socrates said . . .' or 'Socrates says . . .' I mean, Socrates didn't write anything, so all that's left of him is what Plato says about him.

Abel: Plato *says* – that's present.

Barbara: Yes, that's what I would actually say – but can I write it in an essay as well? I do think Plato's still saying something, even though he's dead and the events are in the past.

Abel: And there are different types of event, whether it's present, past or future. There are things that happen, things that happen at a particular time, and things that happen during a period of time. And you have to think about whether the event's over or is still going on.

Barbara: Whoa, slow down a bit! That's too confusing.

5.4.1 Extract from Barbara's essay with confusing tenses

This essay will explore the features of Socratic dialogue to find out whether Socrates is right to call himself a midwife. Some of the features of Socratic dialogues were: they seek definitions of abstract ideas, they cross-examined beliefs to expose contradictions, Socrates used to use questioning to bring the pupil to recognize the truth. Examples for each of these features will be considered and a conclusion has been reached that midwifery could be a good metaphor. The analysis covers the time just before Socrates will be sentenced to death for corrupting youth; this made it particularly poignant that he thought that he may be a kind of midwife.

When Abel underlines the verbs, Barbara can see that she has a mixture of tenses and has not been consistent in her writing. She and Abel agree to see if they can find information in the library and on the Internet that will tell them about tenses. They want to produce a list of different uses in the past, present and future.

The tense of a verb is the form that shows the time of the action. Some writers say that English verbs only have two main tenses – present and past.

Present	Past
It is Sunday today.	It *was* Saturday yesterday.
I write letters on a Sunday.	I *wrote* a letter yesterday.

Think about what these simple sentences tell us about the time and duration of the action or condition. Is it still happening? Is it complete?

Present: It is Sunday today – all day. I regularly write letters on a Sunday. In the simple present tense, the action is something that is here and now. The present tense describes an action or condition that is currently the case or regularly happens and is often used for making general statements, for example: 'He writes very well.'

Past: It was Saturday yesterday and that is in the past. I wrote a letter – the action is over. For the verb 'to write', we only have the forms: write, writes and wrote.

We often want to say more with our verbs than express what is current or what has happened and is over. In some cases, we have to add a helping or *auxiliary verb* to one of the participles – 'writing' or 'written' – or to the *infinitive* – '(to) write'. That's when it starts to get complicated.

For native English speakers, the main problems occur when students don't stay consistently in one set of tenses, usually the present or past. For non-native speakers, there may not be an exact equivalent to the tenses in their own first language and there are some subtle distinctions of usage.

Barbara and Abel have made up a chart of examples of present, past and future uses, based on material they found on the Internet and in grammar books (see the Bibliography for some suggested sources). Barbara intends to use this as a check for her essays until she gets more used to writing them. She has still to decide whether she wants to write in the present or the past about dead authors, but she wants to get to grips with all the possible tenses first. Their chart is shown in Figure 5.2.

It seems to Barbara that there's an unexpected bonus to being able to think about whether things are complete or continuous . . .

5.5 My past, present and future

Barbara:	This is all starting to make sense. I see why you could want a past tense to describe something that's over. That guy Mark – he HAS BEEN my boyfriend but definitely isn't now. I see why they talk about 'has-beens' – it means it's definitely in the past and is no longer.
Abel:	But you HAVE BEEN TALKING to me for the past hour and it is still happening – I hope!
Barbara:	Yeah, but there is a difference. He HAS BEEN a boyfriend uses the past of the verb 'to be'. It's complete – look at the chart, it's a present perfect. But he has been TALKING is a different verb – 'to talk'. It's a continuous perfect – it's still going on.
Abel:	Yes, you're right. I like the idea of something being continuous. We were talking, we are talking, we are going to the pub tonight . . .

> *Barbara:*   Who said we're doing that?
> *Abel:*   I shall have finished my essay by the time you take me to the pub
>   tonight – a future perfect. Sounds perfect to me anyway!
>
> But Barbara isn't listening . . .
>
> *Barbara:*   He is so in the past, that Mark guy. I WENT out with him; I WAS
>   GOING out with him; I HAD GONE out with him before I came to my
>   senses. How far past and over can I make it? Is there anything more
>   past than the pluperfect?

As you can see from Figure 5.2, the auxiliaries are formed from the verbs 'to be' and 'to have'. Another verb is commonly used in this way: 'to do'. It is particularly useful for expressing emphasis or negatives of the simple present or past. It is also useful for questions.

The student *does write* essays well.
The student *did write* an essay last week.

The student *does not write* essays well.
The student *did not write* essays well.
Does the student *write* essays?
Did the student *write* the essay?

Barbara is quite pleased with their chart and sets about revising her essay, to help her practise for next time. She makes the following decisions to help her to be consistent.

Barbara's decisions about tenses (note that other decisions would also have been acceptable):

- The essay exists for the reader, so I'm going to write about it in the present tense. So I'll say: 'This essay explores features of Socratic dialogue . . .'
- Socratic dialogue also exists for the reader, so I'll write about that in the present too: 'Some of the features of Socratic dialogue are . . .'
- If I want to write about something that happened at a specific time, I'd better put that in the past: 'Socrates died in 399 BC.'
- So if I'm talking about Socratic dialogue before Socrates died, I have to decide whether I'm writing about an event that is over and in the past or about the ideas that are still there for the reader to see.
- A mixture of tenses will be OK if I'm clear about whether it's an event that's in the past or a theory that can currently be read.

Go to Section 5.7.5 to see how Barbara rewrote the first paragraph of her essay.

Examples relating to the present

Example	Tense	Usage
The student **writes** essays well.	Present	This is happening now or happens regularly. It is complete.
The student **is writing** the essay now/today.	Continuous present	It may be an action that is currently happening, or it may express intention for the immediate future. This
	(or can be future)	construction suggests that the action happens over a specific period of time and usually refers to visible action.
The student **has written** an excellent essay.	Present perfect	This describes something completed, at an unspecified time. Though the action is in the past, its effect is in the present.
The student **has been writing** an essay.	Continuous perfect	This describes something that began in the past, is still happening and may continue into the future.

Examples relating to the past

Example	Tense	Usage
The student **wrote** an essay last week.	Past	It happened in the past.
The student **was writing** an essay when the fire started.	Continuous past	It happened in the past at the same time as something else.
The student **had written** the essay when the fire started.	Past perfect (*Pluperfect*)	It happened in the past, and was completed before something else.
The student **had been writing** the essay before the fire started.	Continuous past perfect	It began in the past and was ongoing, but was completed before something else.

Examples relating to the future

Example	Tense	Usage
The student **will write** an essay.	Future	It has not happened yet, but will happen in the future.
The student **will be writing** an essay about literacy.	Continuous future	This is continuous action, implying a particular period of time in the future.
The student **will have written** the essay before the tutorial.	Future perfect	It will happen, and be completed before some other future event.
The student **will have been writing** the essay for three months by then.	Future perfect continuous	It will happen, it will be ongoing, it will still be happening at a specified time.

Figure 5.2   Examples of tenses and their usage

Abel's thoughts are more with the future. He is also starting to think about what *might* be, what *could* be and what *ought* to be. Like Barbara, Abel is thinking about his personal life as well as his academic writing; he has some other thoughts relating to what is possible, necessary and obligatory with respect to (a) going to the pub this evening and (b) his relationship with Barbara!

Example	Usage
I *should write* my own essay.	There is a sense of an obligation.
I *ought to write* the essay now.	This also suggests obligations – rather strongly.
I *would write* the essay if I stopped chatting.	Here there is an idea of a condition – something else has to happen as well.
I *can write* the essay.	The student is able to do this.
I *may write* the essay on Newton.	This could express either permission or a possibility – the student is allowed to or it is possible that the student will do it.
I *could write* the essay on Einstein instead.	There is a sense of the student's ability but also an element of uncertainty.
I *must write* a draft of the essay this afternoon.	'Must' expresses necessity, compulsion or obligation (depending on the context).

This introduces a whole range of other auxiliary verbs – notice the subtle differences that Abel can think about. In all of these verbs, the form does not change for the third person (unlike 'he writes the essay', for example). Thus we might say, if it were any of our business:

He should finish the essay today.
He ought to write the essay before going to the pub.
He would write the essay if he stopped thinking about Barbara.
He can write the essay.
He may fall asleep instead of doing the essay.
He could ask Barbara out.
He must phone Barbara before 9 pm or she will be out already.

These verbs are unusual ones. If you are interested in finding out more about them, look up '*modal auxiliaries*' in a grammar book or on the Internet.

Most native English speakers would use these verbs automatically without thinking too much about it. I have mentioned them here to point out that it can be very useful to express levels of ability, certainty, conditions, obligations and necessity. You'll see how useful it is in the final extract from the students' discussions about tenses – how auxiliary verbs can help you to 'hedge' in essays (and other things). *Hedging* means being cautious about claims that you make – which can be important in academic writing, including factual writing. You can hedge using words such as 'possibly' or 'conceivably', or by using particular constructions such as 'It is suggested that . . .'. You can also use some of the auxiliary verbs that Abel has just been considering.

5.6 Facts and possibilities

Barbara and Kim get to the pub first, but Abel has promised to join them when he has written 500 words. Barbara tells Kim about their progress with tenses and shows her the chart in Figure 5.2. Because Kim is studying engineering, she has a different perspective.

Kim: What this? An instruction for a time machine?

Barbara: It's amazing how many tenses there are – ways of expressing different types of time.

Kim: So you've made up a time chart. I wouldn't bother with a lot of that stuff – I just have to give the facts in my writing for uni. And usually it's a report about something that was done, so I keep it in the past.

Barbara: What about quoting from other writers? Or talking about theories?

Kim: Well, I suppose that some things are always true – such as Newton's second law of motion. I'd probably write that in the present tense. Perhaps your time machine chart might be useful. *[Sings]* Let's do the time warp again . . . *[Barbara gives her a funny look.]*

Barbara: I think Abel's writing about Newton.

Kim: Yeah, but he's doing it from a historical perspective – he's probably writing about events in the past.

Barbara: He's analysing Newton's ideas though, so that could be present. Look, here he is now, just in time to get a round in.

Abel looks as though he has a few things on his mind – he does. As well as thinking about Newton, he has an awkward question to ask Barbara. But he's been reading about 'hedging' – using auxiliary verbs that express possibility rather than fact or necessity.

Barbara: Hi Abel – we're talking about tenses. Are you writing about Newton in the past or the present?

Abel: A bit of both – when it's a fact about his life, it's past.

Kim: But his ideas have become facts too, haven't they?

Abel:	Well, I do use the present when I'm talking about his ideas, but I have to watch what I'm claiming to be 'fact'. I find I'm using a lot of hedging.
Barbara:	You're supposed to be writing an essay, not gardening!
Abel:	No – I'm toning things down a bit. Making sure I don't overstate my case. And I'm using some other auxiliary verbs, especially when I'm adding my own interpretations. So I'm saying things like 'Newton could have intended . . .' (because I don't know what he actually intended) or 'Newton seems to be suggesting. . . '. Words like may, might, could or would are very useful for avoiding sounding like a know-all.
Kim:	I use 'it' to do this as well – like, 'it may be the case that . . .', 'it could be interpreted as. . . .'
Abel:	That makes it even more distant.
Kim:	In technical subjects, though some things are facts, you do have to be careful not to make strong claims that might not actually be the case. We have to do quite a bit of hedging. You see it in the books we're reading too.
Barbara:	But if you overdo the hedging, then you end up not saying anything. All these mights and maybes – don't you lose the point?
Kim:	Yeah, when I'm checking I take out some of my vague stuff if I know I can be very definite. But if I find I'm giving a strong opinion, like, 'This result means that our whole life changes' then I usually try and soften it in some way – like, 'it could have a major impact on our lives'.
Barbara:	So you have to avoid being too definite, even with facts.
Kim:	Sometimes.
Abel:	Barbara, I was wondering . . .
Barbara:	Yeah?
Abel:	Could you . . ., would you . . .?
Kim:	*[laughs]* She may, she might, she should!
Barbara:	Shut up Kim. What is it Abel?
Abel:	Barbara – could you lend me a tenner so I can get a round in?

5.7 Comments on questions

5.7.1 Try to find the verbs in the following passage from *Zen and the Art of Motorcycle Maintenance*. Note that the verb might not just be a single word; it may be a phrase.

He was systematic, but to say he thought and acted like a machine would be to misunderstand the nature of his thought. It was not like pistons and wheels and gears all moving at once, massive and co-ordinated. The image of a laser beam comes to mind instead; a single pencil of light of such terrific energy in such extreme concentration it can be shot at the moon and its reflection [can be] seen back on earth. Phaedrus did not try to use his brilliance for general illumination. He sought one specific distant target and aimed for it and hit it. And that was all. General illumination of that target he hit now seems to be left for me.

(Pirsig 1974: 80)

5.7.2 'Write' is a verb: 'writing' and 'written' are what are known as participles. Why do these two words not count as complete verbs?

Both words need another verb to complete them. They can be used as adjectives to describe something (writing style, written work) but need an auxiliary verb if they are going to function as the complete verb in the sentence – I am writing a book; Abel has written an essay.

5.7.3 Should you write an essay using the past tense or the present tense?

Neither would be wrong. It is important to be consistent – decide whether you're using the present or past when referring to writers. The present is rather more manageable, especially when it is necessary to refer to previous events.

Even when you are writing in the present, it is sometimes necessary to indicate that an event is completely in the past – especially if there is a specific time associated with it. An example of this is that Socrates died in 399 BC.

It is also sometimes necessary to indicate that one event preceded – or will precede – another, in which case a mixture of tenses is necessary.

5.7.4 Is 'google' a verb?

It probably is now, though the organization Google was not very happy when this happened. You will 'hear' the characters in this soap opera use google as a verb; I've heard students use 'facebook' in the same way. It is hard to stop such a use.

5.7.5 Barbara's revision to her essay

This essay explores the features of Socratic dialogue to find out whether Socrates was right to call himself a midwife. Some of the features of Socratic dialogues are: they seek definitions of abstract ideas, they cross-examine beliefs to expose contradictions, Socrates uses questioning to bring the pupil to recognize the truth. Examples for each of these features are considered and it is concluded that midwifery could be a good metaphor. The analysis covers the time just before Socrates was sentenced to death for corrupting youth; this <u>makes</u> it particularly poignant that he <u>thinks</u> that he <u>may be</u> a kind of midwife.

Because she is moving between past and present, Barbara decides that it might be helpful to find alternative ways of expressing some of the verbs she is using.

5.7.6 Alternative expression

This revision reduces the number of *finite verbs*.

This essay <u>explores</u> the features of Socratic dialogue to assess the accuracy of Socrates's description of himself as a midwife. Particular attention <u>is paid</u> to Socrates's attempts to seek definitions of abstract ideas, to cross-examine beliefs to expose contradictions, and to use questioning to bring the pupil to recognize the truth. These features <u>suggest</u> that midwifery <u>could be</u> a good metaphor. The analysis <u>covers</u> the time just before Socrates's death sentence for corrupting youth; his idea that he <u>is</u> a kind of midwife <u>is</u> therefore particularly poignant.

5.8 Conclusion: advice about verbs

- A sentence must have a verb. This might be more than one word.
- Complete verbs are of the form play, plays, played. Other forms arise using participles (playing, played) or the infinitive (to play) along with an auxiliary verb.
- Participles are normally formed using -ing (present) or -ed (past). Without auxiliary verbs, they might be used as adjectives.
- If you are puzzled about the tense to use, think about whether the action should be continuous or complete (or both).
- If you think you are making over-strong statements, consider using tenses that suggest possibility rather than necessity.
- When you are checking an assignment, check for consistency.

5.8.1 Technical terms relating to this chapter

For further information, look up these words in the Glossary, other grammar books or the World Wide Web.

Auxiliary verb
Finite verb
Hedging
Infinitive

Intransitive
Modal auxiliaries
Participles
Perfect tense
Person
Pluperfect
Tense
Transitive

6

The complete sentence

6.1 Can students write in sentences? • 6.2 Questions about sentences • 6.3 The sentence as a unit of thought or grammatical structure • 6.4 The sentence and punctuation • 6.5 Sentences and paragraphs • 6.6 Breaking up is hard to do • 6.7 Comments on questions • 6.8 Conclusion: advice about sentences

Falling standards, dumbing down, poor literacy levels: journalists seem to have a lot to say about grammar and language, especially when they are talking about younger people. Our students have picked up a newspaper article that complains about the inability of undergraduates to write in sentences. It seems to them to be the worst form of sneering. But is it true?

6.1 Can students write in sentences?

Abel and Barbara are meeting early to discuss a surprise birthday present for Kim. Abel is reading the paper while he waits for Barbara; she arrives just as he is flinging the paper on the floor. Her bag is getting even heavier; as well as her dictionary, she now has a large book from the library: *The Cambridge Encyclopaedia of Language*. The library's edition comes from 1987. (The full reference is in the Bibliography at the end of this book.)

Barbara: What's up?
Abel: That journalist. Spoonfeeding in schools, he says. Illiteracy.

Students can't write in sentences. Employers complaining about standards. How biased is that?

Barbara: I suppose when I missed out the subject in my essay, I wasn't writing a proper sentence. But that doesn't mean I can't – I just didn't check it properly.

Abel: I know – they say you can't do something, just 'cause you get it wrong once. That makes me mad.

Barbara: Sorry I'm a bit late, Abel. I was getting this book from the library . . .

Abel: Oh, good. Let's see what it says about sentences.

They use the index and eventually find a section on page 94.

Barbara: Oh my goodness, it says there are over 200 definitions of what a sentence is. Well, if we're going to get indignant about newspaper articles, we'll need something a bit more definite than that to defend our case.

Abel: 200 definitions of a sentence! How come?

Barbara: [*Skimming the passage*] Well, it could be to do with a thought, the logic, the grammar, the punctuation, the intonation . . . though I suppose we could rule out some because we're thinking about writing, not speech.

Abel: That's not true, though. Kim's particularly worried about grammar for doing her speech.

Barbara: She's also worried about punctuation. Are we going to get her a book on punctuation, by the way?

Abel: Doesn't sound like a twenty-first birthday present.

Barbara: Well, with other things. Things you can eat, drink, listen to or have a bath in. And we'll look for a jokey book, a friendly one. But not a sneery one. Anyway, she's just coming, so shut up about presents.

Kim joins them.

Kim: You two look very cosy. What are you plotting?

Barbara: Nothing, we're talking about sentences. What do you think a sentence is?

Kim: Something that starts with a capital letter and ends in a full stop and gives me a nightmare in between.

Barbara: I think it's more to do with subjects and verbs.

Abel: Complete verbs – not just bits of them. Not just participles – you know, your favourites, Kim.

Kim: Well, I've got my past participles sorted out now, but I still don't know where to put that full stop. And I also don't know how many sentences you should have before you put a space in.

Abel: From participles to paragraphs. Got a nice ring to it. Participles,

> sentences, paragraphs – I suppose they're all building blocks we're putting in place.

6.2 Questions about sentences

1 How would you define (a) a sentence and (b) a paragraph?
2 What words could you use to join two or more of any of the following sentences to show (a) causation (b) concession? Provide examples of the resulting new sentences.

> Abel is tempted to plagiarize.
> Abel has problems putting things in his own words.
> Abel is keen to write appropriately.
> Abel does not want to be dishonest.

3 Here are some subjects and some *predicates*. Can you find one or more appropriate predicates for each subject?

Abel	
Whoever enters the competition	
I	
Members of the university senate	
The expression 'prizewinning ticket'	
You	

> will be able to choose the prize
> has an equal chance of winning
> hold an important position in the university
> is capable of writing well
> says a lot about the nature of the game
> say that a change is necessary
> are excellent examples of good practice

There are comments on these questions in Section 6.7.

6.3 The sentence as a unit of thought or grammatical structure

A number of definitions of 'sentence' refer to a complete thought or a group of words that make complete grammatical sense. Note that a sentence doesn't have to be true or even make actual sense. Consider: 'The cat has green whiskers.' This is a perfectly acceptable sentence, even if there are no such cats. 'All tulips like gorgonzola.' That's a sentence too, even though it doesn't make much sense at all. It makes grammatical sense: we can follow the structure of it. It helps our understanding to use sensible sentences, however, so we'll start with a few simple ones and then look at some from books.

Some books (for example, Peck and Coyle 1999) refer to the common structure: subject – verb – *object*. Here are some examples:

Subject	Verb	Object
Kim	plays	the saxophone.
The idea	worried	anthropologists.
The competition	will not have	a second prize.

This is a useful starting point; we have already seen the importance of the subject and the verb. The object is the receiver of the action. A verb like 'play' might either take an object or not: 'They were only playing.' is a sentence without an object. Some verbs don't usually make sense without an object though – for example, 'take' or 'have' or 'want'. In these cases, the subject takes or has or wants *something*. Verbs that take objects are transitive – a term we met in Chapter 5.

Peck and Coyle (1999) say that this basic structure frequently helps students to sort out their writing problems. A quick check that each sentence has a subject and verb – and an object if it needs one – usually helps even experienced writers to write more clearly. Of course, the sentences that experienced writers use do get more complicated. In fact, they're not just complicated: they're also compound or complex.

Why should you be bothered to learn about *compound sentences* and *complex sentences*? In Chapter 7, we'll see how they can help you with two of the basic problems with sentences – cutting them in half or running them together.

6.3.1 Compound sentence

A compound sentence is two or more simple sentences joined together with a joining word – *a co-ordinating conjunction*. Here is an example of two simple sentences turned into a compound sentence in various ways.

Simple sentences:

Barbara likes chocolate.
She plans to buy some for Kim.

Compound sentences:

Barbara likes chocolate, and she plans to buy some for Kim.
Barbara likes chocolate, so she plans to buy some for Kim.

The co-ordinating conjunctions are those that are used to combine groups of words of equal weight – two nouns, two phrases, two sentences. Sometimes the *acronym* FANBOYS is used to refer to the seven co-ordinating conjunctions: for, and, nor, but, or, yet, so.

Note that *conjunctions* can also be used to connect smaller units than sentences, for example in compound subjects as we saw in Chapter 4: 'Barbara and Abel are buying a present for Kim.' We can now think about compound objects too: 'Abel will buy coffee and cakes.'

Compound sentences are similarly joining two or more units of equal value. The finite verbs are italicized in the examples below, which are joined by 'but' and 'for' respectively:

Barbara *will buy* chocolate, but Abel *has bought* cakes already.
Barbara *is not buying* it today, for she *might eat* it herself.

6.3.2 Complex sentence

A complex sentence is a simple sentence (or main clause) with at least one *dependent clause*.

A clause is a group of words with a subject and a finite verb. I have already suggested that this is a possible definition of a sentence – and, in fact, another way of describing a sentence is to say that it contains a principal or main clause. Sometimes, however, another clause is added to the main one with a joining word that makes it dependent on the main clause.

There are also conjunctions to join parts of complex sentences. These are known as *subordinating conjunctions* – and there are many more of them. Here are some examples:

after, although, as, because, before, how, if, once, since, that, though, till, unless, until, when, where, whether, while

If you see one of these words, you can tell that there is a dependent clause in the sentence. It depends on the main clause to make sense. It is perhaps easier to understand the idea of a dependent clause through examples. The italicized bits in the examples below are all dependent clauses that link to the main clause through a conjunction. They can't stand by themselves because they have this joining word.

Although Barbara likes chocolate, she will give it away to Kim.
Because Barbara likes chocolate, she thinks Kim will like it too.
If Kim likes chocolate, Barbara will buy it for her birthday.

If you just saw the expression 'because Barbara likes chocolate', you would think it was incomplete. It is dependent on another clause to explain what the connection is that 'because' is making. Sometimes people use incomplete sentences for effect, so you will occasionally see them. But it is better not to do this if you don't understand why it's creating a good effect.

By the way, if anyone ever tells you not to start a sentence with 'because', show them the second example, which is correct according to Standard English. In this sequence, it stresses the reason that Barbara thinks Kim will like chocolate (in this case, drawing attention to the fact that it's not a particularly good reason!). It's rather more common to see a 'because' statement after the main clause, for example: 'Barbara has bought chocolate because Abel says he likes it.' It is certainly not incorrect to do it, but so many teachers have told students that they should never start a sentence with 'because' that it might be safer not to! All you need to do is reverse the sequence so that the main clause comes first.

It is useful to think about the type of dependent clause you are using. In the three examples shown earlier:

1 'Although' is a conjunction that shows concession – even if something is the case, an action will happen that might not be expected. Other examples are 'though' and 'even if'.
2 'Because' is a conjunction that shows the cause for the action. Other examples are 'as' and 'since'.
3 'If' is a conjunction that shows the conditions that will make the action happen. Other examples are 'whether' and 'unless'.

There are other frequently used conjunctions, particularly to do with time and place, for example: 'after', 'since', 'when', 'where'.

Conjunctions are extremely useful for making sentences sound more sophisticated and also for showing where your argument might be going. Think of the useful questions to ask yourself about your main verb: 'where', 'why', 'how' and 'when'. If you can answer any of these, you might have a useful dependent clause; for example: 'Barbara will buy chocolate when she has some money.' 'Who' and 'which' are other interesting questions – used with nouns rather than verbs – and we'll come back to them in Chapter 9 where there is some more to say about dependent clauses.

The sentence, then, may be a unit of thought or a logical relationship between subject, verb and object and it may also benefit from some elaboration. These are quite tricky points; it is worth looking at them in relation to some real pieces of writing. Grammar books, including this one, often use oversimplified sentences as illustrations. Then when you look at real life stuff, it doesn't seem to have any relationship to the examples.

I am using two extracts to make some more points about sentences: one from an engineering book and one from a philosophy book. In each case, I have underlined the subject and emboldened the verb in the main clause of the sentence. Here are some comments on how understanding the grammatical sense can sometimes help the reader to understand the actual sense.

Subjects and verbs: example 1

A branch of analysis, calculus **deals with** rates of changes of functions. There **are** two principal areas of calculus: differential calculus and integral calculus. Differential calculus **provides** a way of calculating maxima and minima of functions and instantaneous rates of changes of functions as opposed to an average rate. With integral calculus, we **are able to calculate** areas and volumes bounded by curves and surfaces with precision, to find lengths of curves, and to determine divergence or convergence of an infinite series of numbers.

(Wright 1994: 163)

Now let's look at each of these sentences in more detail, highlighting subject, verb and object where there is one.

Subject	Verb	Object
1 ... calculus	deals with	rates of changes ...

I am using three dots . . . (an *ellipsis*) to show that I have omitted something. 'A branch of analysis' is an additional description of calculus. It is really part of the subject.
'of functions' gives more detail about the object; it is really part of the object.

Subject	Verb	Object
2 two principal areas of calculus	are	differential calculus and integral calculus (not an object – a complement)

There is no object here; the 'there' construction has been used to set up the subject and there is a complement (the two types of calculus). Note that you could reverse the sentence: Differential calculus and integral calculus are two principal areas of calculus.

Subject	Verb	Object
3 Differential calculus	provides	a way of calculating ...

The rest of the sentence is also part of the object. Note that the object is compound. It's again referring to rates of changes and to functions.

Subject	Verb	Object
4 ... we	are able to calculate ... to find ...	areas and volumes ... lengths ...

Subject	Verb	Object
	to determine . . .	divergence or convergence . . .

'integral calculus' is the topic of this sentence, but is not the subject. 'With integral calculus' is a phrase – an important one saying something about the verb – but the grammatical subject is 'we'.

The 'to' form of the verb, the infinitive, cannot stand on its own but in this case has 'are able' as an auxiliary. This auxiliary does a lot of work here, helping three infinitives, each having an object.

The first and third objects are both compound and there are other ideas to do with curves and series that need to be taken into account.

By separating out the main words in the subject, verb and object we get a clearer picture of what calculus is all about. In missing some words out, I am not denying their importance – they are essential – but I am exposing the structure of the sentence. You might want to try doing this with Example 2 that follows.

Subjects and verbs: example 2

By means of outer sense, a property of our mind, we **represent** to ourselves objects as outside us, and all without exception in space. In space their shape, magnitude, and relation to one another **are** determined or determinable. Inner sense, by means of which the mind intuits itself or its inner state, **yields** indeed no intuition of the soul itself as an object; but there **is** nevertheless a determinate form [namely, time] in which alone the intuition of inner states is possible, and everything which belongs to inner determinations **is therefore represented** in relations of time.

(Kemp Smith 1933: 67)

Here is a similar analysis made for this paragraph from Kant's *Critique of Pure Reason*.

Subject	Verb	Object
1 . . . we	represent . . .	objects

There is a subject, verb and object in this sentence and each is elaborated quite a bit.

The first phrase is itself elaborated with the second phrase – saying how we do the representation. These are phrases rather than clauses as there is no verb.

'to ourselves' is an important phrase following the verb, again saying how we do the representing.

The words after objects say something about objects (which is itself the object of the sentence).

2 . . . their shape, magnitude, and relation to one another	are	determined or determinable (not an object – a complement)

'In space' is an important phrase saying where this happens – it relates to 'are'. Because 'are' is from the verb 'to be', I am suggesting that 'determined or determinable' is a compound complement. If it were just the word 'determined' I would have preferred to talk about this as the passive and put the word in with the verb. In either case, there is no object.

3 Inner sense . . .	yields . . .	no intuition . . .

There is a clause that describes inner sense.
The word 'indeed' is an adverb, emphasizing the verb 'yields'.
'of the soul itself as an object' is an important part of the object.

4 a determinate form	is	time (not an object – a complement)

Note that this is a compound sentence, joined with 'but' as well as a semicolon. It is also a complex sentence, where there is a clause that makes a comment about 'time' – 'a determinate form' that is the subject of the sentence.

5 everything . . . The full subject of the final main clause is: everything which belongs to inner determinations	is . . . represented	(no object)

This long sentence needed the semicolon as well as the 'but' as even the second part of the sentence is itself compound, joined with 'and'.
Though there is no object, the phrase 'in relations of time' explains how the representation is done.
The missing expression after 'everything' is a vital part of the subject. The writer is not talking about everything, but about 'everything which belongs to inner determinations'. Note in particular that there is no comma in this subject. In Chapter 9, I explain why this is important.

The main point here is to keep coming back to:

the verb	what is doing, happening or being
the subject	who or what is actively doing the verb or passively having it done
the object	who or what is the receiver of action of the verb.

If you can understand subjects, verbs and objects, then you can write good sentences. Complements, conjunctions, compound and complex sentences all add to this knowledge. So do phrases and clauses – main clauses and dependent clauses (also known as *subordinate clauses*, because they are joined with subordinating conjunctions). The Glossary at the end of this book defines all of these terms. Don't worry if you haven't understood them all. I had to look some of them up myself to make sure I was using the appropriate expressions!

6.4 The sentence and punctuation

Chapter 10 is devoted to punctuation in sentences; here we are mainly concerned with the notion that a sentence starts with a capital letter and ends in a *full stop*. This is not strictly accurate. There are three ways of finishing a sentence, the full stop being the most common:

a full stop (sometimes called a *period*)	.
a *question mark*	?
an exclamation mark	!

Barbara likes chocolate.
Does Barbara like chocolate?
Barbara is obsessive about chocolate!

For academic writing, you are mostly likely to use the first. You probably should be answering questions rather than asking them and the exclamation mark suggests a sensational use of language that is inappropriate for academic writing.

If you are using any of these punctuation marks, then you will probably have a main clause including at least a verb and a subject. There are other useful marks in sentences – especially commas – and we deal with this in more detail in Chapters 9 and 10. If you find you are using a lot of words in a sentence, to the extent that it is becoming hard to read, you may need to think about punctuation to help you – including using the full stop a bit more frequently. However, at this stage, there is one other punctuation mark to think about with respect to sentences, which is

a semicolon	;

This is a particularly useful mark as it can be used in the same way as a co-ordinating conjunction in compound sentences. That is, it can act instead of a word such as 'and' to link two sentences of equal weight.

Barbara likes chocolate; she prefers it to beer.

In Chapter 7, we'll find out just how useful this can be.

6.5 Sentences and paragraphs

Lecturers hate it when you

- make every sentence a paragraph
- don't use paragraphs.

(Pet hates numbers 6 and 7, from Chapter 1.)

Sentences provide the building blocks for paragraphs, another bugbear for Kim and a source of annoyance for lecturers. It seems that some students make every sentence a paragraph and others don't have any paragraphs at all. Both stem from the same cause; writers don't know what a paragraph is for.

Paragraphs should be visible, either because there are spaces between them or the first word is indented from the margin. The former is now more common, though many textbooks (including this one) still use indentations to indicate new paragraphs. Spacing uses up more paper. If you are not indenting, then you should consider using extra spacing even if your essay is already double-spaced because a paragraph does need to be clearly separated from the next one. You may lose marks unnecessarily if a lecturer can't see where your paragraphs are supposed to end.

I particularly welcome Gowers' (1973) view (see Bibliography), shared by other writers, that paragraphs provide breaks for the reader. This takes us away from the idea of 'what's right' and emphasizes 'what helps', which seems a good principle to follow. The eye gets a rest after a suitable input of information. So a paragraph represents a chunk of information around an idea. If there is a shift in direction, then a new paragraph is necessary. If there seems to be too much to take in, then it is a good idea to look at an appropriate place for a break.

Very short paragraphs suggest a short attention span. You will see them in tabloid newspapers and in children's books, for example. In academic writing, you are more likely to be expanding on a particular point, so if you have a short paragraph you possibly have not said enough about that point. Ask yourself whether you need more evidence, more examples, more details or an alternative perspective.

Often, a paragraph expands on a main statement, sometimes known as a *topic sentence*. This is quite likely to be the first sentence in the paragraph; sometimes it is the last one. The rest of the paragraph gives additional detail around this main point, either expanding from it or building up to it. This is a very useful thing to know; if you have to read a book very quickly, it may be possible to get the gist from reading the first sentence of each paragraph. For example, here is the first sentence (or part of it) from each of the first seven paragraphs of Chapter 17 of Bill Bryson's book, *A Short History of Nearly Everything* (2003).

1 Thank goodness for the atmosphere.
2 The most striking thing about our atmosphere is that there isn't very much of it.
3 For scientific convenience, the atmosphere is divided into four unequal layers; troposphere, stratosphere, mesosphere and ionosphere . . .
4 Beyond the troposphere is the stratosphere.
5 After you have left the troposphere the temperature soon warms up again . . .
6 Even so, spaceships have to take care in the outer atmosphere . . .
7 But you needn't venture to the edge of the atmosphere to be reminded of what hopelessly ground-hugging beings we are.

In general, each of these first sentences is followed by some useful detail. The third paragraph concentrates on the troposphere, which is the first subtheme mentioned in the first sentence, and in this case the most important one. Notice how at the start of paragraphs 4 to 7 there are words that show the change of direction: beyond, after, even so, but. So there is a change of direction with a change of paragraph but it is 'signposted'.

Bill Bryson is an excellent writer, though occasionally his language is slightly more informal than the academic texts you will probably be reading and writing yourself. If we look at his first paragraph, we can see how it expands from the initial topic sentence:

> Thank goodness for the atmosphere. It keeps us warm. Without it, Earth would be a lifeless ball of ice with an average temperature of minus 50 degrees Celsius. In addition, the atmosphere absorbs or deflects incoming swarms of cosmic rays, charged particles, ultraviolet rays and the like. Altogether, the gaseous padding of the atmosphere is equivalent to a 4.5-metre thickness of protective concrete, and without it these invisible visitors from space would slice through us like tiny daggers. Even raindrops would pound us senseless if it weren't for the atmosphere's slowing drag.
>
> (Bryson 2003: 313)

There are six sentences in this paragraph.

1 The topic sentence – an expression of gratitude for the atmosphere. This also an interesting example of a subjectless sentence, though there is an implied 'we'.
2 The first reason for being glad of the atmosphere (warmth).
3 Explanation of the first reason.
4 The second reason (protection).
5 Further elaboration of how we're protected.
6 Further elaboration including implications of not having the atmosphere.

So the whole paragraph expands on why we should be pleased about the atmosphere: it keeps us warm and protects us. This then sets the scene for the next paragraphs, looking at how the atmosphere is formed and how each layer affects us.

Once you become familiar with how paragraphs build up and link together, you'll be able to do it yourself. Don't be afraid just to write things and then organize it into an appropriate sequence and clear paragraphs later.

In the dialogue at the beginning of this chapter, Abel was right to say that we're looking at building blocks. Verbs are at the heart of these and they themselves may be built up.

This seems like a lot to think about, but we put these things together all the time in day-to-day speaking and writing. The analysis is given here to show how it works, not to provide a formula for every sentence you write, as that would take for ever. As always, you are encouraged just to keep writing and then worry about what it looks like through a reader's eyes later. But don't forget this final stage.

6.6 Breaking up is hard to do

Abel has been having one of those 'aha moments'. His building blocks metaphor is helping him in his reading of other people's writing as well as thinking about his own. He has just realized how an abstract or summary captures the main points of a book chapter or journal article. He sees how there is a pattern: identify a theme, say why it is important, say how the topic will be handled in the current piece of writing, have a subtheme as the topic sentence of each of several paragraphs, then conclude by summarizing the most important point that emerges from the piece of writing.

Unfortunately, as so often happens, the aha moment comes at a time when he has other problems. His flatmate, Gus, has 'borrowed' his laptop, though as Abel hadn't given permission, it might be more accurate to say that Gus has appropriated Abel's laptop. Abel knocks on Gus's door:

Abel: Gus – you got my laptop?

Gus: *[Behind the door, silent for a minute]* Sorry mate, I was asleep. What d'you want?

Abel: My laptop. I can't find it and I think you've got it. Hope you haven't messed it up like before. I need to rewrite my essay.

Gus: What you mean rewrite? I thought it was fine.

Abel: This is another one. You know, that I was talking to the grammar pals about.

Gus: Oh them. I wouldn't hang out with them: they're just going to steal all your ideas and you won't get anywhere with either of them.

Abel:	Laptop, Gus – and don't diss my friends!
Gus:	*[Opens door and hands out laptop]* Here it is. Not working properly.
Abel:	I don't believe it. What have you done to it? I need it now – and working. Can't afford to get it fixed; you owe me so much money.
Gus:	Laptop's, like, got a virus, I think. Think about the money as advance rent; I do. So you don't have to pay me anything this month.
Abel:	Know what? I don't think I'll be renting from you for much longer.

6.7 Comments on questions

6.7.1 How would you define (a) a sentence and (b) a paragraph?

(a) This is a difficult question. My own preference is to say that a sentence is a group of words forming a grammatical unit, including at least a verb and a subject. However, I am able to find exceptions to that definition. Other definitions suggest that the group of words should include the expression of a topic, and begin with a capital letter and end with a full stop. Some people define sentences in terms of clauses: a clause is a subject and something that is said about it (also known as a predicate) and a sentence is a group of words with at least one main clause.

(b) A paragraph is a collection of sentences forming a unit. Paragraph breaks give readers a rest and allow them to see when a change in direction is signposted.

6.7.2 What words could you use to join two or more of any of the following sentences to show (a) causation (b) concession? Provide examples of the resulting new sentences.

Abel is tempted to plagiarize.
Abel has problems putting things in his own words.
Abel is keen to write appropriately.
Abel does not want to be dishonest.

These are just examples; you may have thought of others.

(a) Causation

Abel is tempted to plagiarize because he has problems putting things in his own words.

Abel is keen to write appropriately, so he is tempted to plagiarize.

(b) Concession

> Although Abel does not want to be dishonest, he is keen to write appropriately and is tempted to plagiarize.

> Even if Abel is tempted to plagiarize, he does not want to be dishonest.

6.7.3 Here are some subjects and some predicates. Can you find one or more appropriate predicate for each subject?

Answers to this question might have been formed by (a) what you believe is the truth, (b) what is possible grammatically, (c) what makes sense. The suggestions below have been filled in on a grammatical basis, taking some account of possibility (what can be said about 'an expression'). There may be some predicates that you believe are not appropriate from the point of view of 'the truth'. The predicate – what is said about the subject – has to use an appropriate form of the verb to match the subject.

Abel	will be able to choose the prize
	has an equal chance of winning
	is capable of writing well
	says a lot about the nature of the game
Whoever enters the competition	will be able to choose the prize
	has an equal chance of winning
	is capable of writing well
	says a lot about the nature of the game
I	will be able to choose the prize
	hold an important position in the university
	say that a change is necessary
Members of the university senate	will be able to choose the prize
	hold an important position in the university
	say that a change is necessary
	are excellent examples of good practice
The expression 'prizewinning ticket'	says a lot about the nature of the game
You	will be able to choose the prize
	hold an important position in the university
	say that a change is necessary
	are excellent examples of good practice

6.8 Conclusion: advice about sentences

Students can – and do – write in sentences all the time. A few errors keep recurring. The following points may help you to avoid these common mistakes.

- Get used to the structure of subject, verb, object.
- Use conjunctions to make your sentences more elaborate.
- Paragraphs should give readers a break.
- There is often a topic sentence at the start of a paragraph.

6.8.1 Technical terms relating to this chapter

For further information, look up these words or phrases in the Glossary, other grammar books or the World Wide Web.

Adverbial clause
Clause
Complex sentence (see Figure 6.1)
Compound sentence (see Figure 6.1)
Conjunction
Co-ordinating conjunction
Dependent clause
Ellipsis
Object
Predicate
Subordinate clause (another word for dependent clause)
Subordinating conjunction
Topic sentence

1 Simple sentence

You might also see this called a principal clause, a main clause or an independent clause. There is often an object, but not always.

2 Compound sentence

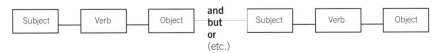

3 Complex sentence

Figure 6.1 Building blocks of sentences

7

What goes wrong with sentences?

7.1 Too much or too little • 7.2 Questions about sentence errors • 7.3 How to avoid running sentences together • 7.4 How to avoid chopping sentences in two • 7.5 Sentenced to death! • 7.6 Comments on questions • 7.7 Conclusion: advice about fixing sentences

No wonder students can't write in sentences: they're complicated. But the basic structure given in Chapter 6 and especially in Figure 6.1 can help to work out where they are going wrong. There are basically two problems: sentences are run together or sentences are incomplete.

7.1 Too much or too little

Kim is finishing off a draft section that is due with her tutor in three days. She normally asks her flatmates to check her work over, but three of them are about to go off on a three-month placement and are too busy to help. That's another thing; she is going to need to find some flatmates. She starts to wonder if either Barbara or Abel would like to be a proofreader or a flatmate. And then there are the invitations for the party. Should she treat them as a couple? It's all too much. Just as she is thinking about them, they arrive at her door.

Kim:	Come in – I was just thinking about you both.
Barbara:	Good stuff, I hope. I came to ask you a favour and bumped into Abel here, looking like a wet weekend.
Abel:	I need a favour too. I need to borrow a computer to finish off my assignment. Gus has given mine a virus. He's getting to be a real pain.
Barbara:	And I thought I'd see if you'd swap writing with me. There's something about my sentences that doesn't sound right. I've stopped my participles dangling – sounds rude that, doesn't it? But the grammar checker still thinks something's wrong with them.
Kim:	Not sure that I can help. But I was looking for someone to check my stuff. Let's swap and see what happens. There's too little time to get everything done. Abel, you can use my computer, if there's no virus on your flashdrive.

7.2 Questions about sentence errors

1 What are you likely to find too much or too many of if sentences are run together?
2 What is likely to be missing if sentences are incomplete?
3 Here is an extract from Barbara's essay. Which 'sentences' are ungrammatical? (Think about subjects and verbs.)

> Speech acts happen when we 'do things with words' (Austin 1962) argues that by using certain words, someone might be making a promise or launching a ship. Launching a ship is dependent on the context in which the words are said. With a range of alternative explanations, such as acting in a play about launching a ship or parodying someone who is launching a ship. This essay explores the extent to which any utterance might be described as a speech act. Looking in particular at speakers' intentions and unintended effects.

4 Here is an extract from Kim's report. Which sentences are ungrammatical?

> To utilize the effects described by Bernoulli, Euler and others, air-flow has to be deflected in order to produce a pressure differential. Air will flow round an obstruction speeding up to do so airstreams tend to create an aerofoil shape round an obstruction. The fact that this happens can be exploited to maximize the lift effect of the aerofoil shape, the airstream gets separated because of the obstruction and the air on one surface has to travel further and faster than the air on the other.

There are comments on these question in Section 7.6.

7.3 How to avoid running sentences together

A recurring problem with student essays is that sentences run together. Very often, a student puts in a comma, because 'it sounds like a short pause'. When you have two main clauses a comma is not (usually) strong enough to separate them. I can always think of exceptions in elegant writing, but the use of the comma to 'splice' two sentences is generally unacceptable and considered a particular fault in student writing. You may remember it was number 10 in lecturers' pet hates in Chapter 1.

There are several reasons why a comma splice happens. I have identified some typical ones in Figure 7.1. I have provided a possible correction. Below, I have summarized the approaches I have taken in this figure to avoid using a comma splice.

Here are some alternatives to comma splices:

1 Rewrite the sentences to reduce the number of main clauses.
2 Substitute the subject of a clause with a linking word (typically change 'this' to 'which') and keep it as one sentence.
3 Use a semicolon before words such as 'however' or 'therefore' that introduce new main clauses.
4 Put in another full stop to separate the sentences.
5 Turn one of the sentences into a dependent clause.

Although the comma splice is one of the most common ways of running sentences together, it should be noted that *run-on sentences* can happen without commas too! This is why it is so useful to understand about finite verbs and their subjects. If you have two finite verbs and two subjects, you need some devices to avoid running them together. These devices might have different functions for the sentences:

Co-ordinate	with a word like 'and', 'but', 'so' or a semicolon
Subordinate	with a word like 'when', 'because', 'although'
Separate	with a full stop

Subordinate clauses are another name for dependent clauses and we'll be looking at them in more detail in Chapter 9. If you subordinate a clause then you make it lower in rank – that is, you don't allow it to be a main clause, but it says something about the main clause.

Reason	Typical 'wrong' sentence using a comma splice	Possible correction
1 The writer is unaware that there are two main clauses.	This essay is about cause and effect, it argues that the relationship does not have to be mechanical.	This essay argues that the cause and effect relationship does not have to be a mechanical one.
2 The writer does not realize that 'This' is a subject rather than a linking word.	It is important first to look at the way we use language, this affects how we understand the nature of causes.	It is important first to look at the way we use language, which affects how we understand the nature of causes.
3 The writer thinks that 'however' should be used as a conjunction to join two main clauses. (It should not.)	If one event occurs immediately after another there may be a causal connection, however, there may be no necessary connection between them at all.	If one event occurs immediately after another there may be a causal connection; however, there may be no necessary connection between them at all.
4 The writer has got so carried away with the message that the sentence has not stopped.	We have discovered that there is a difference between sufficient and necessary conditions, there is also a difference between causally necessary and logically necessary conditions.	We have discovered that there is a difference between sufficient and necessary conditions. There is also a difference between causally necessary and logically necessary conditions.
5 The writer has not identified a subordinate relationship for one of the two clauses.	We may need to retain the idea of the Causal Principle, science as we know it could not operate without it.	We may need to retain the idea of the Causal Principle, because science as we know it could not operate without it.

Figure 7.1 Comma splices and how to avoid them

7.4 How to avoid chopping sentences in two

The other main problem with sentences comes when they are not complete. They are not sentences at all, even if they follow the rule 'Start with a capital letter and end with a full stop.'

Number 5 of the lecturers' pet hates in Chapter 1 was when students write sentences without verbs. This would clearly be one of the causes of an incomplete sentence. It is not the only one, however. We have already seen that as well as a verb, a sentence needs a subject. So if a sentence is missing a verb or a subject, then it is likely to be incomplete. The result is sometimes called a 'sentence *fragment*' (Figure 7.2); if you get a message from a grammar checker that you have one of these, then check your subjects and verbs. Again, there are a number of reasons for a sentence fragment.

Some alternatives to sentence fragments, then, are the following:

- Use a *colon* to separate the main clause from an explanation.
- Bring the fragment back into the previous sentence. Use a comma to separate a subordinate clause from a main clause.
- If the fragment is long, or hard to relate to the previous sentence, put in a subject and a finite verb.
- Make sure that any commentary has a subject and a finite verb.

So it's not so much that people don't finish their sentences, it's more often the case that they put the ending into a new sentence. The incomplete bit often follows on from a complete sentence. In fact, it ought to be a subordinate clause.

Again, what is really important is to make sure that you have a main clause with a subject and verb and to create appropriate links or separation from other clauses.

Reason	Typical sentence fragments (underlined)	Possible correction
1 The writer thinks a full stop is needed as there would be a significant pause in speech.	There was a significant event that influenced Galileo's thinking about how the universe works. The invention of the telescope.	There was a significant event that influenced Galileo's thinking about how the universe works: the invention of the telescope.
2 The writer does not realize that 'which' is a linking word rather than a subject.	Galileo noticed that four small 'stars' near Jupiter were in fact revolving around the planet. Which contradicted astrology and religion.	Galileo noticed that four small 'stars' near Jupiter were in fact revolving around the planet, which contradicted astrology and religion.
3 The writer thinks that a present participle is sufficient action in the sentence; however, a present participle is an incomplete verb.	Copernicus had earlier suggested that the earth moved round the sun. Convincing Galileo at an early age, though he kept quiet about it at first.	Copernicus had earlier suggested that the earth moved round the sun. This had convinced Galileo at an early age, though he kept quiet about it at first.
4 The writer wants to make a brief observation, without explicitly stating an opinion.	Galileo realized that the teachings of Aristotle and the Church were inaccurate. A dangerous view.	Galileo realized that the teachings of Aristotle and the Church were inaccurate. This proved to be a dangerous view.

Figure 7.2 Sentence fragments and how to avoid them

7.5 Sentenced to death!

Barbara, Abel and Kim have been through a few grammar books and put together some observations about sentences, a bit like the ones here and in Chapter 6. They'd like to write a reply to the journalist who said that students can't write in sentences, but after all their efforts, they don't know where to start.

Barbara: If you look at what the lecturers have marked in red, most of the time our sentences are fine. Just occasionally, we run them together or chop them up. I chop 'em up – but I know why. It's the way I speak and hear it in my head. I think it's just a matter of checking.

Kim: I run everything together – sentences, paragraphs etc. – so I can get it all down. Then I throw in a few commas. But I will start looking for subjects and verbs; it's not that difficult.

Abel: I probably haven't been pulled up for it so much because I used to copy the sentence structure from the books I was using! But I was nearly in trouble for plagiarism, which is much worse.

Kim: But it's useful to think of that. You can copy sentence structure without plagiarizing, as long as you're not using the same ideas. So copy the shape of the sentence, but have a different subject, different verb.

Barbara: Yes, I need to use more signpost words like 'although' and 'however'. I'm going to look for other examples – see how the books do it.

Abel: Signposts – you mean, words that point to where the argument's going. I like that idea. I'm going to try that too.

Kim: So – we sometimes make mistakes, 'cause we don't check enough or we haven't been aware of some things. Doesn't mean we *can't* write sentences – we write loads of them. But I've had enough of sentences – I'm sick of 'em. I've just got one more for you; I'd like you to come to my party.

She hands Barbara a card.

Abel: Don't I get an invite?

Kim: One per couple. These cost a fortune to print. And it's the last time I'm saying or writing the word 'sentence' today.

You have been found guilty of being considered OK by Kim. Your sentence will be to attend:

A Rocky Horror Birthday Party

20 May from midnight
(after the showing of the
Rocky Horror Picture Show)

Bring a ghoul if you want.

7.6 Comments on questions

7.6.1 What are you likely to find too much or too many of if sentences are run together?

Too much punctuation could suggest a problem, especially lots of commas, dashes and semicolons. It may even be that the grammar is correct, strictly speaking, but the reader has lost the will to live by the end of the sentence. The sentence is definitely ungrammatical if there are two main finite verbs without any co-ordination – a conjunction or semicolon.

7.6.2 What is likely to be missing if sentences are incomplete?

The most likely element to be missing is the verb or perhaps a part of the verb, where participles need another verb to be complete. Sometimes, it is the subject of the sentence that is missing. This is why it is useful to get into the habit of thinking about subjects and verbs.

7.6.3 Here is an extract from Barbara's essay. Which 'sentences' are ungrammatical? (Think about subjects and verbs.)

I have italicized the wrong sentences.

Speech acts happen when we 'do things with words' (Austin 1962) argues that by using certain words, someone might be making a promise or launching a ship. Launching a ship is dependent on the context in which the words are said. *With a range of alternative explanations, such as acting in a play about launching a ship or parodying someone who is launching a ship.* This essay explores the extent to which any utterance might be described as a speech act. *Looking in particular at speakers' intentions and unintended effects.*

The first sentence needs to be two sentences. Barbara is trying to use her reference to act as the subject of a new sentence. A subject cannot be in *parentheses* like this. She is more likely to split sentences, though. Both the other wrong sentences are lacking a finite verb (the -ing form is incomplete) and a subject. Her second sentence is correct though. 'Launching a ship' is the subject and the verb is 'is'.

7.6.4 Here is an extract from Kim's report. Which sentences are ungrammatical?

To utilize the effects described by Bernoulli, Euler and others, air-flow has to be deflected in order to produce a pressure differential. Air will flow round an obstruction speeding up to do so airstreams tend to create an aerofoil shape round an obstruction. The fact that this happens can be exploited to maximize the lift effect of the aerofoil shape, the airstream gets separated because of the obstruction and the air on one surface has to travel further and faster than the air on the other.

Kim's first sentence is correct; the other two contain two sentences run together.

7.7 Conclusion: advice about fixing sentences

Students can – and do – write in sentences all the time. A few errors keep recurring. The following points may help you to avoid these common mistakes.

- If it sounds wrong, perhaps it needs a subject and a finite verb – or has too many of these without connections.
- A comma followed by 'this' or 'however' may be a sign of a comma splice.
- A sentence that starts with 'which' may be a fragment.
- A verb ending in -ing is not complete and needs an auxiliary to be in a main clause.

7.7.1 Technical terms relating to this chapter

For further information, look up these words or phrases in the Glossary, other grammar books or the World Wide Web.

Comma splice
Compound sentence
Conjunction
Fragment
Run-on sentence

8

Speaking personally

8.1 Having a voice

Barbara has invited the others round to her flat as Abel's computer is still
broken. Abel has been running his latest essay through the grammar checker
on Barbara's computer. When he gets to the sentence, 'Galileo was considered
to be a heretic and was brought to trial by the Inquisition', the checker
announces, 'There appears to be a verb in the passive voice.' Abel starts
shouting at the computer.

Abel: Speak English, why don't you! What's passive?
Kim: The passive's OK – I use it all the time in my reports. It saves me
           having to say 'I'. So instead of saying, 'I calibrated the microm-
           eter' I say, 'The micrometer was calibrated'. It gets rid of me
           altogether – some people might think that's a good idea!
Abel: Is that why they call it voice? You've got no voice – no real say in
           what you're writing? That's what it feels like to me; we get it in
           science too – if I calibrate it, why shouldn't I say so? But I wasn't
           avoiding 'I' here anyway.
Barbara: I suppose it is about whose voice you're hearing. In your sentence,

you could have said the Inquisition considered Galileo a heretic and brought him to trial. Then you'd have been hearing the Inquisition's voice – well, at least getting the sentence more from their point of view.

Abel: But I wanted to emphasize Galileo and what was done to him.

Kim: Think about that, though – it's a good way of putting it. You use the passive when you want to emphasize what happens to something or someone. And you use the active when you want to emphasize what something or someone does.

Barbara: So active's like, 'I hate that guy Mark' and passive's, 'That guy is hated.' Well hated, in fact, and not just by me! So I'd use the passive if I wanted to say more about him than me.

Abel: That makes sense. But I don't think you should say any more about him anyway. [Quickly moving on] I got pulled up for saying, 'I have found no scientific evidence' when it was the evidence, or lack of it, that I wanted to highlight. So, 'No scientific evidence was found' would be better – and it takes me out of the picture.

Barbara: What about, 'There is no scientific evidence'? Wouldn't that be better?

Kim: Well, it would be OK if you could say for certain that Abel's looked at all the possible evidence. The speed he's working at just now, I don't think that's likely.

Abel: That sounds like a sneer, Kim.

Kim: But not a grammar one – it's a reflection on your practice. Actually, I think you're right to say, 'No scientific evidence was found.'

Barbara: Well, I still think mine's better – 'There is no scientific evidence . . .'

8.2 Questions about personal expression

1   How can you tell the difference between the active and the passive?
2   Why do some grammar checkers object to the passive while some lecturers love it?
3   Which is the better impersonal version of 'I have found no scientific evidence . . .' – Abel's version or Barbara's?
4   Do professors, tutors or lecturers want students' opinions?
5   Why do academic staff talk about reflective writing and what do they want?

There are comments on these questions in Section 8.9.

8.3 Reasons for using the passive

Grammar books report the following reasons for using the *passive voice*: (1) to emphasize what was done to something or someone; (2) to be impersonal; (3) to avoid giving a person's identity, either because it is unknown or inappropriate. These reasons can be seen in the following examples:

1 Socrates was accused of corruption.
2 The literature has been reviewed for information on social policy.
3 The ship was torpedoed during the war.

In each case, further information might be available by adding an expression after the verb beginning with the word 'by': 'by the Athenian Assembly'; 'by the author'; 'by the British Navy'. When this happens, it actually counteracts the original reasons for using the passive – it highlights the identity of the people who did the action. So it is possible to use the passive to draw attention to an individual agent, as well as to avoid doing this.

The passive is often used in official writing or speech. 'Customers are requested not to smoke.' 'Passengers are reminded that passports are required.' This avoids having to say who is requesting, reminding or requiring.

Grammar books also suggest that you should avoid the use of the passive if possible. The active is more direct and easier to read. There are ways of making even neutral academic writing more active. To take the example of the literature review, here are some alternative approaches, still neutral but using the *active voice*:

Active but impersonal:

The literature on social policy provides some useful background to this issue.

A review of literature on social policy follows this introduction.

The first stage of the project has involved a review of literature on social policy.

In the first and second examples, it is obvious that the author has made a review of the literature and just wants to get on and say why it was important. In the third one, the author is keen to specify that he or she has completed a literature review.

8.4 When passives get awkward

The passive is usually formed with part of the verb 'to be' and the past participle.

> The dog ate the bone. (Active)
> The bone *was eaten*. (Passive)
> The dog is eating the bone. (Active)
> The bone *is being eaten*. (Passive)

You can find passives in almost any tense, but there are some cases where rewriting would be preferable. For example, you can interchange the following sentences:

> The student writes essays well. (Active)
> The essays *are well* written. (Passive)

However, if you try to change 'The student has been writing an essay' to the passive, it gets a bit messy. 'An essay has been being written' doesn't sound right at all. You might want to say something like: 'An essay has been started.'

Some verbs do not translate well into the passive voice. Think of Martin Luther King's famous statement:

> I have a dream. (Active)

'A dream is had' just wouldn't sound idiomatic. If Martin Luther King had not wanted to use the first person, he might have used an expression such as:

> There is a dream. (Passive)

It would have worked grammatically, but would definitely not have been so powerful!

The following example shows another type of problem:

> I have tried to give evidence for my main findings. (Active)

You certainly might want to make this passive to get rid of the 'I'. But you don't want the findings to 'have been tried to be given'! It would be better to say:

> An attempt has been made to give evidence for the main findings.
> (Passive)

You should always remember that there are other possible ways of writing anything. Rather than tie yourself in knots trying to turn an 'I' expression into a passive, you might find a better way of putting it. For example, the passive example above might be better as:

> Where possible, the report contains the evidence for the main findings. (Active, but impersonal)

Some people think that the passive is nearly always awkward. It is becoming quite a contentious topic.

8.5 When people get awkward

All this talk about the passive voice has made Kim feel rather active. She has been looking through one of her engineering books and has found that it uses the passive voice throughout.

Kim:	Look at this – the body is constrained, the table is shown, the forces are applied, the transformation has been described . . . no wonder I've found it all so hard to follow.
Barbara:	It's just as bad in philosophy – ideas are derived, causes are attributed, identity is postulated . . .
Kim:	Well, you'd expect philosophy to be vague, but science and engineering should be precise. So it should say who or what is doing the constraining or applying the forces. I think I'm going to use active verbs right throughout my own project.
Abel:	But it won't be neutral enough if you do. You can't just start shoving 'I' in – the engineers hate it.
Kim:	No, but it must be possible to write things in plain English.
Barbara:	I don't think philosophy's vague – it's trying to be precise too.
Kim:	And when I do my presentation, I'll use a lot of active verbs for that. It's OK to use 'I' and 'we' in presentations. And the active verbs will be much better for speech.
Barbara:	I think I'm too passive myself – I just let things be done to me, instead of being the person who's doing things.
Kim:	Well, go and do something useful, like get us the biscuits. I've got a talk to write. An active one. And it's going to be full of my opinions!

8.6 Expressing an opinion without saying 'I'

We saw in Chapter 2 that Abel agonized over whether he should refer to himself as the author, one or I. The passive voice is one way of avoiding this – but there can be other ways. I am frequently asked by students, 'Do they want my opinion?' My answer is that tutors do want your opinion; they would just rather you didn't say it that way.

Students frequently want to write 'I believe that . . .' or 'It is my opinion that . . .'. If you find you have written an expression like this in your first draft, then score out these words. You will be left with a statement. Then you should consider whether you have any evidence or good reasons for making such a statement.
Here are two examples:

(a) Poverty is a major cause of ill-health.
(b) Falsification is not necessary.

In example (a), the student might look for statistics or other evidence from books to back up this claim. It may be necessary to tone it down a little by saying something such as: 'Statistics suggest that there is a strong association between poverty and ill-health.' You would also have to include a reference to your source of information for these statistics.
In example (b), the student might end up with a statement such as: 'Falsification may not be necessary for scientific progress because alternative explanations can still arise without it.' In this case, the student (such as Abel) is giving a reason rather than evidence, though it still might be useful to add some examples if he can.

8.7 Bring me back: reflective writing

Just as students are starting to get used to avoiding 'I', some academics are encouraging them to write reflectively. This may not sound particularly relevant to a book on grammar, but a couple of reviewers of the first edition of the book said they were concerned that students have difficulties with reflective writing. In fact, I think it *is* relevant because it is all tied up with what people feel they are 'allowed' to say. This context is very important for thinking about appropriate grammar and language use, as we also saw in Chapter 2.
Being able to identify the subject of a sentence encourages you to think about who or what is in control of a situation. This is significant for students

because you are expected to be in control of your own learning and work at university. In recent years, there have been various initiatives to promote this. One you may have heard of is 'personal development planning' (*PDP*). All universities in the UK are providing opportunities for students to do some structured reflection on their own learning. This has had a greater impact in some subject areas than others; many of the professional subjects have been encouraging people to reflect on their own abilities, to evaluate their progress and to plan for their future. Many people are now expected to do this throughout their entire working life.

A very useful way of doing this kind of reflection is to keep a journal or log – again, some courses will ask for this. Some logs can be entirely factual, but a reflective one involves making judgements about what you have done as well as just describing it. Such a document might be structured according to some questions or checklists given to you by your department. Alternatively, you might be entirely free to 'go with the flow' – something that some students find very difficult after many years of being told exactly how to do things.

If you are asked to write a reflective piece and have not been given any guidance, try jotting down answers to the following questions:

1 What did I do?
2 Why did I do this? Or why was I asked to do this?
3 How did I approach the task?
4 What happened?
5 What does this say about me?
6 What does it say about the context?
7 What would I do differently next time?
8 What are the main messages from this activity?

There are many more potential questions like this. The most useful are the ones that you think up for yourself.

If you are stuck with your writing, one very useful technique is *freewriting* (see Elbow (1973) in the Bibliography at the end of the book). This is great for people who have felt constrained by grammatical rules, or exhortations about how you 'should' write. In freewriting, you just write for a short time (say 10 minutes) without stopping. Then later you can think about what the writing is telling you. Many people find out what they are thinking by using this technique frequently.

Barbara has been doing something a bit similar: she's been blogging.

8.8 Reflections on what's going wrong

Extract from Barbara's blog: 'Confessions of a first year student'

> What's going wrong?
>
> Everything! I can't get my sentences to work out, Mark still hasn't got back in touch, and I don't know what to do about Abel. Kim has given me an invitation to her party for Abel and me, but I think I want to take Mark if I have to take a partner. I was starting to write this about grammar and look how it's turned into talking about Mark; I thought I'd been good about this. But I'm making so many connections, about being active instead of passive, making sure that I am the subject of my own sentences. Of course, I also made the connection about Mark being very much in the past. So perhaps I'm contradicting myself.
>
> And I have to write a reflective piece for tomorrow on the process of writing my essay. This is supposed to help avoid plagiarism, I suppose, because if you've just plagiarized you won't be able to reflect on the process. I suppose that I can make some observations about making a first draft and rewriting my essay; I know that I have got better at recognizing what is happening and this is by paying attention to grammatical structures when I am reading and writing. It has been so helpful to get someone else's point of view – a reader's perspective – on the sentences that I'm writing. I'm becoming aware of the need to see what I am saying from a reader's point of view . . .
>
> A few more lines in this vein and Barbara discovers that she almost has a basis for the reflective piece she has to write. She hits 'publish blog' and then gets to work on her homework. It is only later that it occurs to her that she has made her continued interest in Mark rather too public by putting it on an unrestricted blog. That causes Barbara some further reflection!

There is a serious point here: some students believe that the encouragement to be reflective can be quite personal. You need to be careful not to interpret the demand for reflection as an intrusive request to reveal personal information that you would rather keep to yourself. People are very different in this respect.

8.9 Comments on questions

8.9.1 How can you tell the difference between the active and the passive?

You are looking at the action in the sentence. Where is the emphasis? Is it on what someone or something is doing (active)? Or is the emphasis on what is done to them?

Active	The students gave a presentation.
Passive	The students were given a standing ovation.

The passive is usually formed with a part of the verb 'to be' and the past participle.

8.9.2 Why do some grammar checkers object to the passive while some lecturers love it?

The passive voice is more difficult to follow. People often criticize it for hiding the identity of the person who is doing the action. Some lecturers like the passive voice, however, because it encourages neutral language, especially avoiding 'I'. It focuses on what has been done rather than on who did it.

8.9.3 Which is the better impersonal version of 'I have found no scientific evidence . . .' – Abel's version or Barbara's?

'There is' or 'there are' are useful expressions if you want to be impersonal: for example, 'There are several possible ways to explore this topic.'

In this example, however, Barbara's claim that 'There is no scientific evidence' is a very strong one. An experienced lecturer who has read the main works on a topic might be able to make such a claim (and they frequently do); Abel is probably safer just to say that 'No scientific evidence was found', or he could hedge and say: 'There is apparently no scientific evidence . . .'.

8.9.4 Do professors, tutors or lecturers want students' opinions?

They say that they don't, but they usually do. They want to know what you think is important in your selection of what to write. When you present the evidence for your argument, you are giving your own take on the topic, even when that involves bringing in a lot of other people's opinions. They tend not to be keen on unsupported opinion: so you should be getting into the habit of asking yourself, 'What evidence and what reasons do I have for making this claim?'

8.9.5 Why do academic staff talk about reflective writing and what do they want?

There has been a strong move in recent years to encourage students to evaluate their own learning processes and reflect on the experiences that they have been having. A graduate is someone who makes well-informed judgements; by encouraging you to articulate how you are responding to your studies, your tutors help you to become someone who can make judgements on personal actions, achievements and aims, a notion tied up with professionalism. Departments vary in how specific they are about this; if your own is not too helpful, there are some useful books around (see especially Cottrell (2003), listed in the Bibliography).

8.10 Conclusion: advice about personal writing

- The passive voice uses a form of the verb 'to be' along with the past participle, for example: 'The problem *is described* below.'
- It is particularly used in neutral impersonal writing and where the emphasis is on what is done to the subject rather than on the person or thing doing it (the agent).
- Don't feel that you have to change your sentence just because the grammar checker says it's passive.
- However, it is sometimes worth asking whether active verbs would be preferable.
- It's not always necessary to do a straight translation between active and passive; often there is a better way of saying the same thing.
- If you want to express an opinion or make a claim, then think about your reasons and evidence.
- You should make sure that you know whether you need to do any reflective writing or personal development planning; most courses in the UK have an element of this.
- Try just writing without stopping; you can always rewrite it later. It's OK to write rubbish at any time (just don't hand it in!).
- If you are asked to write reflectively or personally this does not mean that you are expected to make your private thoughts and feelings public. It is up to you how much you reveal.
- Nevertheless, to gain most benefit from the activity, you should take it seriously and not just make up what you think 'sounds' good.

8.10.1 Technical terms relating to this chapter

For further information, look up these words in the Glossary, other grammar books or the World Wide Web.

> Active voice
> Freewriting
> Passive voice
> PDP
> Reflective writing
> Voice

9

More on complex sentences: relationships and relatives

In this chapter, we look more closely at how to expand a simple sentence using dependent clauses. In Chapter 6, we saw how conjunctions could be used to create clauses that were dependent or subordinate to the main clause. There are other kinds of subordinate clauses too, with different types of link. In particular, students often have problems with what are called 'relative' clauses – and our case study shows some problems with other kinds of relatives as well (brothers).

Relative clauses act like adjectives; they say something about a noun in the sentence. In the story, they say something about brothers, but it could easily be something else – such as photosynthesis or postmodernist thought!

9.1 Talking about relatives

Kim has a lot on her plate just now. She has a reason for wanting to sort out her sentence structure that she has not yet explained to Barbara and Abel and she's beginning to feel uncomfortable about keeping secrets from them. This is particularly difficult as Barbara is staying in her flat for a while, because her own has developed some unpleasant leaks.

It's just as well that Kim is in a large flat and that her flatmates have now gone on a three-month placement. Kim comes from a big family and two of her four brothers have decided they want to stay with her for a few days before her party. She has masses of coursework to do, especially as she is in her final year. Her dissertation and her presentation are particularly worrying her. She's finding herself distracted by some of the grammar issues and she's also seen a competition she wants to enter with a laptop for a prize, because she needs a new one. The competition involves writing a romantic short story – it's not her sort of thing, but she thinks she'll give it a go.

And, of course, she has a party to organize. She doesn't really know much about *The Rocky Horror Picture Show*, but it had seemed like a good idea at the time when she heard that the film was coming to town. The discussion about tenses (Chapter 5) had got her singing the 'time warp' song, so she blames that.

Today Kim has a meeting with her tutor at 4.30 pm, she's supposed to be going to a football game at 6 pm with Barbara and Abel, and her brother Derek from Dundee has announced that he'll be arriving in time to go to the football too. She might not get back to the flat in time to meet Barbara and Abel. She leaves a note for Barbara:

> I've gone to see my tutor. My brother, who comes from Dundee, will be coming with us to the football. I'll meet you there.

Barbara is multitasking: she is eating chocolate, doing some reading for her project, and thinking about why Kim gave her and Abel a joint invitation as a couple. The doorbell goes at about 5.15 pm. When she answers the door, there is Abel and a guy that looks a bit like Barbara's type (though she admits herself that that covers quite a wide range).

Abel: This is Kim's brother – just met him outside. He's come to stay.
Barbara: Oh, that's great. She did leave me a note. You have to come to the football with us. What's your name? I'm Barbara.
Eddie: I'm Eddie. I think I'll just wait here if that's OK. I've got some papers to read. I'm a law student – got a dissertation due in.
Barbara: No, no, she said you had to come. I've got to take you. I think we'd

better go now in fact. The road's busy and there aren't many buses. I'm ready – just dump your bag and we'll get going.

Barbara bustles Abel and Eddie out and they get to the football match in good time. Kim is waiting for them at their usual place and she's got another man with her, who also looks like he might be Barbara's 'type'.

Kim: Hi, Eddie – goodness, Barbara how did you persuade him to come? He hates football. This is Derek, my brother from Dundee. I met him off the train.

Barbara: I thought Eddie was your brother!

Kim: He is. Eddie is my brother who lives in Edinburgh. You're probably going to meet Harry tonight as well. Harry's my brother who's still from around here – like me, he didn't move very far from home. And my other brother, Jack, who is coming to the party too, is building a house in Newcastle. So soon he'll be my brother who comes from Newcastle.

Barbara: But your note said your brother would be coming with us.

Kim: My brother who comes from Dundee.

Eddie: And your brother who likes football. I'm your brother who doesn't and who has a dissertation to write. I'm your brother who got hijacked by your bossy flatmate.

Barbara: I think there was something wrong with your note. It would have been easier if you had given his name. Then your brother Eddie, who is obviously too clever to go to football games, could have stayed at home.

Abel: Can someone tell me what is going on?

Eddie: It's her relative clauses. Kim never knows whether she's defining or describing her relatives.

9.2 Questions about relationships and clauses

1 Here is a set of *relative pronouns*. Can you put the correct ones in the sentences that follow? (There may be more than one possible correct answer.)

who, whoever, whom, whose, which, what, that

This is the house . . . Jack built.
Abel did . . . he could to finish his essay.
The brother . . . comes from Dundee is Barbara's favourite.
The brother . . . bag is still in the flat wants to go back now.

Kim's favourite person, . . . pays for Eddie's ticket, will be rewarded with a beer.
Kim can't be too hard on Barbara from . . . she has borrowed £10.
Kim is having a party, . . . will happen next weekend.

2   What is the difference between the following two pairs of sentences? How do the commas change the meaning?

Your brother, who is too clever for football, is going home.
Your brother who is too clever for football is going home.

Students who reflect on their practice have the most success.
Students, who reflect on their practice, have the most success.

There are comments on these questions in Section 9.7.

9.3 Words expressing relationship

If you are a native English speaker, you probably did not have too much difficulty with Question 1 above, though there were a couple of possible traps. I wondered about bothering you with the information that these words are called 'relative pronouns', but I have decided that it is useful because the label might draw attention to what is going on here. If there is a relative pronoun, it needs something to connect to in the sentence.

These little words can often result in problems in students' writing. We saw in Chapter 7 that the relative pronoun 'which' is sometimes used mistakenly as the subject of a sentence. Another kind of pronoun, 'this', should be used instead. The following sentences illustrate the different uses.

I have a birthday party to go to, which will cost me a lot of money.
I have a birthday party to go to. This will cost me a lot of money.

Some of the words we are using here can also be used as pronouns to start questions. A lot of words in English can be used in more than one way and this does cause some confusion.

In the examples in Figure 9.1, however, we are thinking about the words as relative pronouns – words that introduce a certain type of clause – and there are a few things that can be said about using them correctly. A pronoun is used as a substitute for a noun; when it is relative, it *relates* to another noun or pronoun in the sentence.

To see if you can understand this, can you find the noun that each example in Figure 9.1 relates to?

	Meaning, example and notes
who	This means 'the person or people which'. It is used of people, where 'which' is used of things. **The people who are entering the competition have a week to write their story.**

whoever	This is more general: it refers to 'everyone who' or 'whatever person'. It is similar in use to whatever, wherever etc. Sometimes, 'ever' is used after 'who' in other ways, and this causes some confusion.
	  1 **The winner of each section, whoever writes the best story of its genre, will receive a laptop.**
	  2 Who ever saw such beautiful people?
	(In the second example, 'who' is a different kind of pronoun – interrogative – and does not belong here.)

whom	People often worry about whether they should use 'whom'. It is used when 'who' becomes the object of the sentence. **She is the person whom I contacted about the competition.** Nowadays, the word is often not used when it might sound stilted. Above, it could be omitted or replaced with 'that'.
whose	This is a *possessive* for both 'who' and 'which' – in other words, it doesn't just need to apply to people. **The company whose competition Kim is entering lays great stress on good writing.**
which	'Which' is the relative pronoun used of things rather than people. **Kim is entering the competition, which closes a week on Friday.**
that	'That' can be used to replace 'who' 'whom' or 'which', especially if it is defining something. Grammar checkers on computers often suggest 'that' instead of 'which' especially if there is no comma before it. It is not necessary to make this substitution, though some people prefer it. **Barbara wants to know about the competition that Kim is entering.**
what	Although 'what' can be used as a relative pronoun, it should not be used to replace 'which' (though this is quite common in some dialects). It can be used for 'that which' or 'those which', for example: **Kim is studying for what she hopes is her last exam.**

Figure 9.1   Relative pronouns

The nouns for each relative pronoun are:

who = people   which = competition
whoever = winner   that = competition
whom = person   what = exam
whose = company

9.4 Revisiting the subordinates

Before we look in more detail at how we can use these relative pronouns, I want to come back to the idea of clauses. This section reviews what I have said about them already, and extends the notion of subordinate or dependent clauses.

Chapter 6 considered three types of sentence: simple, compound and complex. These are summarized below.

9.4.1 Simple sentence: What's the action and who or what is the subject of it?

There is one main clause, with a subject and verb. It possibly includes adverbs, adjectives and other nouns (e.g. object or complement). The example below has a subject, verb, object and adverb.

Abel plays tennis regularly.

9.4.2 Compound sentence: What actions and subjects have equal importance and can be joined together?

There are two or more simple sentences joined with a conjunction. 'But' is a conjunction that links or co-ordinates two sentences where one has a contrasting meaning to the other.

Abel plays tennis regularly but he has gone to the football game today.

9.4.3 Complex sentence: What can we say about the action, subject or object?

A comment is made on the main clause, with a subordinate or dependent clause. 'Although' is a conjunction that indicates that there is something to say about the main clause, in this case admitting that something is different to what might be expected.

Abel plays tennis regularly, although he has gone to the football game today.

We saw that conjunctions could act as 'signposts' to show the answers to the questions like how, where, why and when. Now we can add two more questions – what and who – and use relative pronouns to introduce other subordinate clauses.

Abel plays tennis, which he prefers to football.
Abel, who plays tennis regularly, is fitter than Derek.

These clauses act like adjectives – that is, they describe a noun, such as tennis and Abel.

'What' can also be used to create clauses that work like nouns.

Abel believed what Kim had told him about Barbara's feelings.

In this case, the clause acts as the object of the sentence.

Subordinate clauses, then, can act in the same way as:

adverbs	saying how, why, when and where something happened
adjectives	saying something about a noun or pronoun in the sentence
nouns	being a subject, object or other noun or pronoun

Remember, a clause always has a verb in it and that verb will usually have a subject. A subordinate clause expands the main clause in some way. It is also known as a dependent clause, showing that it depends on the main clause.

> I am not a grammarian. To me a subordinate clause will for ever be (since I heard the actor Martin Jarvis describe it thus) one of Santa's little helpers.
>
> (Truss 2003: 32)

So if even Lynne Truss doesn't want to know about them, why should you bother about subordinate clauses? Well, knowing about subordinate clauses can help you to write more complex sentences accurately and to 'signpost' your writing. It is also useful to know what they are so you can get rid of them if you have too many.

Now that we have added 'who' and 'what' to the way we can expand our main clauses, it is perhaps worth bringing together some of these linking words as a set of potentially useful expressions for essays and reports. Some of the examples in Figure 9.2 can also be used for phrases rather than clauses – and, in fact, too many clauses can cause problems.

You can often replace subordinate clauses with simpler expressions, without verbs. If your sentences are getting complicated, with too many subordinate clauses, think about simplifying the clauses into phrases.

- while the investigation was happening – during the investigation
- because there is insufficient evidence – because of insufficient evidence
- . . ., which will be a method for testing the hypothesis – . . ., a method for testing the hypothesis

So I'm not necessarily encouraging you to use a lot of subordinate clauses. They can be the cause of the 'convoluted' sentences that were lecturers'

To show...	Example link words	Some subordinate clauses
when	after, before, until, when, while	while the investigation was happening
where	where, wherever	wherever the incidents have occurred
why	as, because, since	because there is insufficient evidence
what	which, that	which will be a method for testing the hypothesis
who	who, whose, that	whose research has made a significant contribution
what conditions are necessary	if, unless	if the tests prove positive
concession	although, even if	although many writers agree
comparison	as if, like	as if the opposite had been the case

Figure 9.2   Subordinating and signposting

number 8 pet hate in Chapter 1; they may also be related to number 9 about pompous language. And I've already pointed out that knowledge about clauses can help you avoid number 5 (sentences without verbs) and number 10 (run-on sentences).

But subordinate clauses do have their uses. The next section considers two of these: defining and describing.

9.5 Relative clauses: defining and describing a brother

In this chapter, I am particularly interested in relative clauses. This is not just because Kim has so many relatives: it is also because the confusion at the football match showed two different types of relative clauses (see Figure 9.3). I am sure you realize that you don't have to be talking about brothers to use relative clauses; however, Kim's brothers do bring out the distinction between these two types. As Eddie pointed out, Kim needs to be sure whether she is defining or describing her brother.

Note that if you were speaking the two sentences in the examples in Figure 9.3, the intonation would be slightly different in each.

In the case of defining, the meaning might have been clearer if it had been used in a contrast between the two brothers.

My brother who comes from Dundee will go to the game, but my brother who comes from Edinburgh hates football.

	Example	Notes
Describing	My brother, who comes from Dundee, will go to the game.	In this case, the expression 'who comes from Dundee' is an additional part of the sentence. It is not essential to the meaning, but is an aside. We can tell this because commas have been used to enclose the expression. (In Chapter 10, we look in more detail at the use of commas for enclosing.)
Defining	My brother who comes from Dundee will go to the game.	Here, the expression 'who comes from Dundee' has not been separated off as a description. It defines which brother is being

Figure 9.3   Relative clauses that describe or define

Again, it should be noted that the whole situation would be much simpler and clearer without unnecessary verbs:

My brother from Dundee will go to the game, but my brother from Edinburgh hates football.

Sometimes, however, we do need a relative clause that defines or restricts a noun or pronoun. In Chapter 6, we saw the expression from Kant's *Critique of Pure Reason*:

everything which belongs to inner determinations

There I made it clear that the clause 'which belongs to inner determinations' was a necessary part of the subject of the sentence. The clause is not a description of 'everything'; it is a definition of what is covered by 'everything'.

This is a tricky distinction and Chapter 10 returns to it, to emphasize the importance of punctuation. But our students have found another problem with relative clauses that define and describe: should they be using 'which' or 'that'? I should point out that I wouldn't be mentioning this at all if grammar checkers didn't make such a fuss about it!

9.6 Every which way but that

Back at the flat, Eddie has decided to forgive Barbara for dragging him to the football, but only because he wants to borrow her dictionary and get her to help proofread his dissertation. Barbara is rather grumpy because she thought he had been rude to her because of a simple misunderstanding over commas. She'd also rather talk to Derek than think any more about grammar. You may notice this in her responses.

Eddie: Can you just read this sentence; there's something funny about it.

Barbara: Well, it doesn't make me laugh. It just sounds wrong. Why are you saying 'that' here? 'The author, that spent his placement in Fife, acknowledges the support of three local legal practices.' 'That' refers to things, not people, surely. Well, of course you may have a point . . .

Eddie: No, I've been told that 'that' can refer to people too. Especially in restrictive clauses.

Barbara: In what?

Eddie: Restrictive clauses. I don't know what that means though. Can you look it up in your dictionary?

Barbara: [*Sighs*] OK. Restrictive. [*Reads from Chambers Dictionary*] It says here: 'expressing restriction, as in relative clauses, phrases etc. that limit the application of the verb to the subject'. Look, it gives an example – very appropriate: '*People who like historic buildings should visit Edinburgh.*'

Eddie: Oh, so it's like, defining.

Barbara: Yes, people who like historic buildings – and no commas. And yes, you probably could say 'people that like historic buildings . . .'. It's like in the definition: 'phrases that limit the application' – there you could say 'which' instead of that.

Eddie: Ah, then I'm not right because it's not restrictive. It's descriptive: it should be 'The author, who spent his placement in Fife . . .'. It's just that the grammar checker keeps telling me to replace 'which' with 'that'. And I knew you could replace 'who' with 'that' sometimes too.

Barbara: [*Annoyed*] You're making my head spin. And it sounds suspiciously like the same point you were making about brothers from Dundee and Edinburgh. Are you sure you know what you're talking about?

They go and borrow a couple of Kim's grammar books and put together the information that can be seen in Figure 9.4. Barbara added the examples: she said she was fed up with types of clauses having so many different names and it's easier to remember examples. (I tend to agree with her!)

Eddie: So grammar checkers aren't always right.
Barbara: And neither are you.

Use...	Example
which for things in descriptive or *non-restrictive* clauses	This book, which I have found helpful, is due back at the library.
who for people in descriptive or non-restrictive clauses	The lecturer, who had a PhD, knew the answer to my problem.
which OR **that** for things in defining or restrictive clauses	The book which is overdue must be returned immediately; you can keep the other one. OR
(use **that** if you want to keep the grammar checker quiet!)	The book that is overdue must be returned immediately; you can keep the other one.
who OR **that** for people in defining or restrictive clauses	The lecturer who had a PhD knew less than the other one. OR The lecturer that had a PhD knew less than the other one.

Figure 9.4   Which or that?

It is important to let you know about this. I have heard of cases where lecturers, perhaps influenced by grammar checkers, insist on 'that' instead of 'which' in cases where the clause is defining the subject. Current grammar books suggest the attitude is old fashioned; it is probably a case where the language is going through a change. It is as well to know that people have different views on this. The problem with the grammar checker is that it is not always able to tell what your context is. There will be more on this problem in Chapter 12.

9.7 Comments on questions

9.7.1 Here is a set of relative pronouns. Can you put the correct ones in the sentences that follow? (There may be more than one possible correct answer.)

who, whoever, whom, whose, which, what, that

This is the house *that* (or *which*) Jack built.
Abel did *what* he could to finish his essay.
The brother *who* (or *that*) comes from Dundee is Barbara's favourite.
The brother *whose* bag is still in the flat wants to go back now.

Kim's favourite person, *whoever* pays for Eddie's ticket, will be rewarded with a beer.
Kim can't be too hard on Barbara from *whom* she has borrowed £10.
Kim is having a party, *which* will happen next weekend.

In the last example, 'that will happen next weekend' doesn't actually sound wrong and I suspect that some writers (for example, Palmer 2003) would be quite happy with it.

9.7.2 What is the difference between the following two pairs of sentences? How do the commas change the meaning?

Your brother, who is too clever for football, is going home.
Your brother who is too clever for football is going home.

Students, who reflect on their practice, have the most success.
Students who reflect on their practice have the most success.

In each case, the clause in the first example is descriptive and not an essential part of the subject of the sentence. In the second examples the clause is used to specify the people referred to. This can make quite a difference to the meaning. With commas, there is a suggestion that all students have the success, presumably compared to groups of people who are not students. Without commas, the reference is to a particular subset of students. The latter is more likely to be correct in this case.

This chapter has spent some time on the distinction between describing and defining, which Chapter 10 will revisit.

9.8 Conclusion: advice about relative clauses

- Use 'who' (or 'whom', 'whoever' or 'whose' as appropriate) for people and 'which' for things.
- You can replace 'who' or 'which' with 'that' in *restrictive clauses*, though you don't have to.
- Think about whether you want your clause to describe (*non-restrictive clause*) or define (restrictive clause); you don't need to remember these names, but you do need to know where to put the commas.

9.8.1 Technical terms relating to this chapter

For further information, look up these words in the Glossary, other grammar books or the World Wide Web.

- Adverbial clause
- Non-restrictive clause
- *Noun clause*
- Phrase
- *Possessive*
- Relative clause
- Relative pronoun
- Restrictive clause
- Subordinate clause

10

How to be offensive with punctuation

10.1 Define without using commas

Kim and Barbara are having some toast in the flat before going to university and the mail arrives. Kim's brother Eddie, who went back to Edinburgh to hand in his dissertation, has sent her a letter. He has a special message for Barbara, but Barbara doesn't get to that bit as when Kim shows her the letter she is so incensed about the third sentence (Figure 10.1).

Kim: Pompous git. Who writes letters these days? Why not just send me an email? Do you want to see it?

Barbara: Oh, I like getting letters. I think it should be encouraged; it's more personal. But yeah, let's see it.

Kim: Here you are – there's a bit about you in it anyway. He seems to have taken a shine to you – it's not like him! I'd better tell him you're spoken for.

Barbara: What do you mean? I'm not spoken for. *[She starts to read.]* Oh, that's ridiculous. Look what he's saying about English football fans. I'm English. I really object to that, Kim!

Kim: I just skimmed over that bit. Yes, I see what you mean. That's pure racist. Especially when we know he knows what he's saying. He knows about relative clauses – we talked about it.

Barbara: Who'd have thought that two little commas could be so offensive?

Kim: It does make me think that punctuation matters. I didn't used to think that it did.

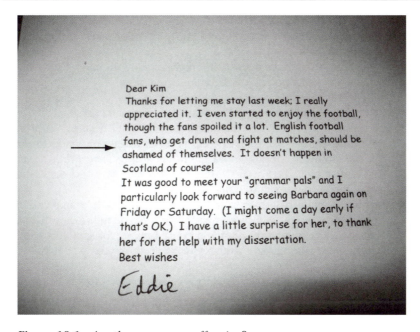

Figure 10.1 Are these commas offensive?

10.2 Questions about punctuation

1 Do you think the sentence in Eddie's letter is more offensive with or without commas? Why?

2 This question relates to the joke behind the title of Lynne Truss's book (*Eats, Shoots and Leaves* – see Bibliography).

What are the main differences between the two pandas:

(a) The panda eats shoots and leaves.

(b) The panda eats, shoots and leaves.

3 If you look for other punctuation jokes on the Internet, the main one you find is a version of the following. A professor asked a class of students to punctuate this sentence.

   Woman without her man is nothing
   (a) How did the boys punctuate it?
   (b) How did the girls punctuate it?

4 Punctuate the following sentences so that any ambiguity – which may even be offensive – is removed. In most cases, you'll have to put in punctuation but you may need to take some out as well.

   (a) Abel laughed and joked about failure an hour after Barbara failed her exam
   (b) What a mess you have made a difference already though
   (c) I've got a friend who could ask for anything more
   (d) When Kim plays the piano sounds out of tune
   (e) I'll give Kim, a bag, a box of chocolates and a birthday card
   (f) Kims birthday presents are the following a DVD of the *Rocky Horror Show* the theme for her party cakes, iced with her teams colours to improve her punctuation; a book and a comic recording *Phonetically Speaking* by Victor Borge a bedroom scene a painting she likes chocolates and a bag to hide other unwanted presents
   (g) Isnt that touching Barbara said Abel have you seen the bloke you used to go out with his friend is Kims brother Welsh friends are here too it seems we've got plenty of men if youre looking for someone new Im not the one I want already knows who she is dont you

There are comments on these questions in Section 10.7.

10.3 The functions of punctuation marks

The main function of punctuation is to support meaning. It shows us how a group of words should be read together. It lets us know where to stop and what to keep separate. It may tell us that a group of words is an aside: for example, a description or a comment. It may even tell us that there is something missing. If you have any doubts about the value of punctuation, here is a well-written paragraph with the punctuation removed, along with the capital letters that indicate a new sentence. You might want to consider where the punctuation marks should go. (The untampered version is in Section 10.7, after the comments on the questions.)

There are I suppose only a few works that seem even more essential to the Western Canon than *Paradise Lost* Shakespeares major tragedies Chaucers *Canterbury Tales* Dantes *Divine Comedy* the Torah the Gospels Cervantes *Don Quixote* Homers epics except perhaps for Dantes poem none of these is as embattled as Miltons dark work Shakespeare undoubtedly received provocation from rival playwrights while Chaucer charmingly cited fictive authorities and concealed his authentic obligations to Dante and Boccaccio the Hebrew Bible and the Greek New Testament were revised into their present forms by redactionists who may have shared very little with the original authors whom they were editing Cervantes with unsurpassed mirth parodied unto death his chivalric forerunners while we do not have the texts of Homers precursors

(Bloom 1994: 26)

Many people (not everyone), seeing such a passage, would try to work out which words go with which. Sometimes it is quite easy to do this; sometimes you need a little help. This is what punctuation is for: to help you to work out which words go together and how they would sound if they were said out loud.

For some people, the words go together like music – they hear a set of words in their heads as they might hear a set of notes that naturally go together. We use the same word for this process, with both words and music: phrasing.

When Kim realizes this, the penny drops. She has been practising the saxophone to play at her party and suddenly she is aware that she is thinking about punctuation as she is playing the piece.

Kim: 'Let's do. The time-warp. A-gain.'
Well, it might punctuate the music but it makes a bit of a mess of the sentence if you're saying it normally. But yes – it is almost the same thing. The musical notation tells you where to stop, where to pause, what bits go together, where the emphasis goes. That's all it is. I need to turn my sentences into music!

Kim realizes that she's talking to herself and goes off to find Barbara and Abel. Barbara is still staying with her and Kim thinks Abel might be there too (in fact, he's been hinting about moving in), but he's out playing tennis. Barbara is at the kitchen table dreamily moving around sticky notes (Figure 10.2). She has written words on each and is trying them out in different sequences. Kim reads some of these.

Kim: You've got hundreds of these. What on earth are you doing?

Barbara:	I've been going through some books looking for useful expressions for essays. There are loads of them; I've been using them already whenever I'm stuck for something to say.
Kim:	They seem to be bits of sentences: phrases and clauses.
Barbara:	Yes – they're words that go together, but they still need to be put with main clauses. It's like Abel was saying about building blocks. I haven't really thought about words working together before.
Kim:	I was just thinking about that with music too . . .
Barbara:	I heard you!
Kim:	. . . and I think it might help with punctuation. You know, sometimes you have to stop. Sometimes you need to separate out bits that go together, like phrases. Sometimes you're almost saying 'here's a little aside'. There are signs in music to help you with these things; I suppose punctuation's a bit like that too.
Barbara:	I don't know what you're talking about. I don't read music or anything like that. But I can see the same thing with these sticky notes. Some of these are words I want to keep together. And then I might need to make it clear that they belong to each other and are separate from another bit of the sentence.

The doorbell rings, and Abel is standing there flushed after his game of tennis, but he starts talking almost as soon as Kim opens the door.

Abel:	It was hard to concentrate on the game, 'cause I kept thinking about punctuation! Each rally was like a sentence and the lines of the court turned into commas or full stops. If you were outside the line, you had to stop and start again. It was like a new sentence!
Barbara:	I think you've both gone mad. Punctuation is about words, not tennis movements or musical notes!
Kim:	Well, we each have our own ways of thinking about things. And it doesn't hurt anyone. But we're all talking about stopping things, separating them . . .
Barbara:	Making little asides.
Kim:	. . . and interrupting what I'm saying. I think Abel and I are thinking about rhythms, and you're more interested in the way things look.
Abel:	Different learning preferences. You need to think about that if you're a teacher. So some kids would be more likely to remember things they hear and some things they see. Or even do. So you have to vary the way you teach them.
Barbara:	Is there any point to this?
Kim:	Yes – lots of points. Punctuation points. I've just never thought about what they're for. Let's put them together and see what we come up with.

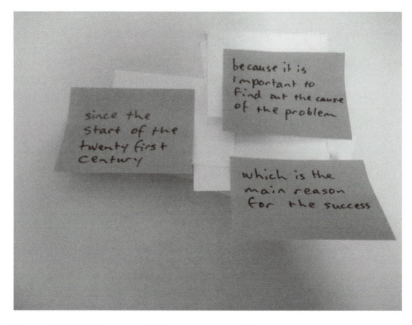

Figure 10.2   Phrases and clauses may need punctuation

Using some of the language books they've been looking at, the students try to identify the different functions of different punctuation marks. The result is in Figure 10.3 which shows punctuation in its role within sentences. It looks at marks by function: completing, introducing, separating, enclosing and omitting. These are the main things that you have to do in sentences. Now that you have these examples of functions, try taking a few sentences from a book and see if you can say whether each punctuation mark completes, introduces, separates, encloses or omits.

There are some other punctuation marks too, which do things within individual words rather than sentences. They are used for abbreviations (full stop and apostrophe), joining (*hyphen*) and omitting (apostrophe). We look at these briefly in Section 10.5. We'll be taking a closer look at the apostrophe in Chapter 11 – it's so important that it has been given a chapter to itself.

Completing
You must have one of the following at the end of each sentence.

Mark	Name	Function	Example
.	Full stop or period	Marks the end of a sentence.	The two writers interpret the same information in very different ways.
?	Question mark	Marks the end of a question.	What methods are available for analysing such data?
!	Exclamation mark	Ends a sarcastic or emphatic statement. (Best to avoid.)	Readers can make what they want of that statement!

Introducing
Use one of these to introduce a distinctive part of the sentence

Mark	Name	Function	Example
,	Comma	Introduces direct speech.	One student reported, 'I think I have done enough to pass.'
:	Colon	(a) Introduces a list, after a word that sums it up.	Lecturers have several complaints: poor punctuation, poor sentence structure, inadequate paragraphing, and wrong use of words.
		(b) Introduces a quotation or direct speech (as an alternative to a comma).	Mark Twain said: 'When angry, count a hundred; when very angry, swear.'
		(c) Introduces an explanation or particular example.	There is another punctuation mark that you should know: the apostrophe.
–	Dash	Indicates a change of direction, or significant follow up.	This view of the world was accepted for centuries – then Newton made his important discovery.

Figure 10.3   Functions of punctuation marks in sentences

Separating

Use one of these to separate parts of a sentence.

Mark	Name	Function	Example
,	Comma	(a) Separates a phrase or dependent clause, especially if it comes first.	Because the essay was late, the student got a reduced mark.
		(b) Separates items in a list.	The main consequences of failure of this equipment are accidents, delays, loss of material, and financial penalties.
		(c) Separates direct speech from the speaker. Note that the comma is before the quotation mark.	'I think I have done enough to pass,' she said.
;	Semicolon	(a) Separates items (e.g. in a list) that already contain commas, or are quite long.	The study considered three main areas of research: the effects of frequent use of drugs; the roles of the mother, father and siblings in the behaviour of the young person; the impact of custodial sentences on reoffending.
		(b) Acts as a conjunction.	The third theory was tested first; it was thought the easiest.

Figure 10.3 continued   (*Continued overleaf*)

Enclosing
To enclose information in a sentence, use one of these pairs.

Mark	Name	Function	Example
, ,	Commas	Separate an aside or extra phrase that the sentence does not need grammatically.	The result, which was a surprise, was a win for our team.
( )	Parentheses	(a) Indicate an aside that is interesting but not very important.	We discovered (as did previous citation to provide researchers) that consistency was crucial to the study.
		(b) Used in some forms of information given in more detail in the references.	According to Chandler (1995), academic writers adopt various different strategies.
[ ]	Square brackets	(a) Often used to insert editorial/explanatory comments on another's writing.	The student claimed: 'We benefited most when our TMA [tutor marked assignment] was returned to us within a week.'
		(b) Can be used in numerical referencing systems.	The findings by the first researchers [16] were quite unexpected.
– –	Dashes	Separate with more emphasis than commas.	The third group – all mature students – demonstrated the most unusual approach to the project.
' ' " "	Quotation marks/ *inverted commas*	(a) Enclose direct speech. Use single or double, but be consistent.	McLuhan said, 'The medium is the message.'
		(b) Highlight the first use of an unfamiliar word or phrase	This type of drawing is usually known as a 'free body diagram'.
		(c) Indicate the title of a chapter or journal article	Bartholomae, D. (1985). 'Inventing the university' in M. Rose (ed.), *When a Writer Can't Write*. New York and London: Guilford Press.
	Scare quotes	(d) Draw attention to a word or phrase. Don't overuse.	This 'prediction' turned out to be false.

Figure 10.3 continued

Omitting

To show that something is missing, use the appropriate one of these.

Mark	Name	Function	Example
...	Ellipsis	Trailing off a thought. Missing word(s). Useful for quotes. The example uses what the writer thinks is important, but shows there were other words.	Smith (1999) said: 'Students … will use a range of intelligences.'
——	Long dash (Printers would call it a two em dash)	A name or other word is omitted.	A study was undertaken at —— University to find out about students' grammar.

Figure 10.3 continued

10.4 Putting punctuation to work

The comma is one of the most common punctuation marks, and it does cause some confusion. This is possibly because it has three of the five roles: it introduces, separates and encloses. Mistakes can happen if it should be enclosing but one of the commas is missing, for example. Alternatively, people may think that they need to enclose something but are not sure what should be enclosed and put a comma in a wrong place. Then it can separate things that should be left together! The advice to read a sentence aloud and pause slightly when you come to a comma is generally useful (though not foolproof).

Sometimes there is disagreement among experts as to whether a comma is necessary. Some say that it is essential before the conjunction in compound sentences (see Chapter 6 – Section 6.3.1); others don't think it is necessary if the meaning is clear. I would be happy with either:

Barbara is studying now and she will go out later.
Barbara is studying now, and she will go out later.

The word 'she' could also be omitted in either case. I would definitely want a comma to aid the reader in:

Students must be prepared to take risks, and their tutors need to help them through this.

Without the comma in that sentence, there could be a suggestion at first reading that students need to take their tutors as well as risks!

As well as being necessary for understanding, punctuation is used by skilful authors to create an effect. Here is a passage from an old edition of Charles Dickens's *Pickwick Papers*, where an eccentric character called Mr Jingle, a rascal, has a very distinctive way of speaking. The punctuation helps us to 'hear' his voice, which gives us more information about his personality. The long dash usually indicates omissions or interruptions. Dickens has stretched this convention to convey Jingle's jerky and incomplete speech.

> 'Ah! You should keep dogs – fine animals – sagacious creatures – dog of my own once – pointer – surprising instinct – out shooting one day – entering inclosure – whistled – dog stopped – whistled again – Ponto – no go; stock still – called him – Ponto, Ponto – wouldn't move – dog transfixed – staring at a board – looked up, saw an inscription – "Gamekeeper has orders to shoot all dogs found in this inclosure" – wouldn't pass it – wonderful dog – valuable dog that – very.'
>
> (Dickens 1837/1963)

While you wouldn't write an academic work in such a way, it is useful to see how punctuation contributes to the meaning. Notice as well that the whole passage is in single inverted commas, but Jingle wants to quote something himself so that statement has to go into double inverted commas. (It doesn't matter which way round you do this as long as you are consistent.) We shall say more about use of inverted commas in Chapter 13.

10.5 Punctuation within words

The hyphen has several functions, but its main one is to ensure that the reader doesn't get confused (Figure 10.4). There are also some conventions to observe with hyphens. The main one is to connect words that are used together as an adjective. This happens only before a noun, not after it. For example:

Kim has an up-to-date project.
Kim's project is up to date.

The main change with hyphens is that they are tending to disappear. But they are still necessary in some cases to avoid confusion.

Possible confusion	Example use	Comments
A word is split over two lines of type and the reader needs to know that it continues.	We want it to be read-able for everyone.	'readable' is one word. Someone seeing 'read' and 'able' on two different lines might try to read the sentence differently. A wordprocessor can be set to do this hyphenation for you. It will break a word in an appropriate place, usually at the start of a syllable.
	However, DON'T split expressions like the following …	
	Today you were not-able by your absence	It would be better to avoid such breaks,
	There was need for the-rapists.	even with a hyphen.
Without the hyphen, the word already has a meaning.	re-covering	= covering again (e.g. furniture)
	recovering	= getting or finding again
Without the hyphen, it is not clear which words should go together.	lead-free petrol	petrol without lead
	lead free petrol	Is this petrol that costs nothing?
Without the hyphen, a compound word looks strange, especially if it is a new expression.	e-book	As expressions become part of the language, they often lose the hyphen. It sometimes becomes a matter of personal preference: e.g. either e-book or ebook would be acceptable now.
Without the hyphen, there may be too many of the same letter in a word.	shell-like	The word 'shelllike' would look very odd because of the triple l.

Figure 10.4   Using a hyphen to avoid confusion

The full stop or period used as an abbreviation is also tending to disappear. It is now quite rare to see it used in expressions such as:

Mr.   abbreviation for Mister

Mrs. abbreviation for Mistress, pronounced 'Missus'
Dr.   abbreviation for Doctor

We are so familiar with these terms of address that we no longer need to show that there are letters missing. But it is not wrong to do so.

It is still quite common to see full stops in abbreviations such as e.g. or i.e., though even these are increasingly seen without them. These are abbreviations for Latin expressions and students find them quite useful, though they often use them the wrong way round. Make sure you know what they mean:

e.g.   exempli gratia   for example
i.e.   id est   that is

It is probably better to avoid the abbreviations in formal text anyway and just write 'for example' or 'that is' as appropriate. In general, the advice is to avoid abbreviations.

Both the hyphen and the full stop (used for abbreviations), then, are used less than they used to be. As an expression becomes familiar without one, then we tend to miss out the mark. As always, if in doubt it is useful to check a recently published dictionary.

10.6 A dodgy colon and a full stop

Time is getting very tight for Kim. She's making notes for her talk to the industrial sponsors, hearing the rhythms of her own speech in her head as she writes. It's flowing quite well. Barbara and Abel are sitting together in the next room proofreading her dissertation: Kim hopes that this will bring them closer together. Unfortunately, her romantic notions about them are not helped by the fact that Abel is feeling unwell and Barbara is just irritable. However, their conversation contains some useful observations about punctuation.

Abel: I've had an idea for the title. What do you think, Barbara? 'Vibra-
           tions, colon, minimizing and avoiding them.'
Barbara: We're proofreading, Abel, not editing. Leave her title alone – there's
           nothing wrong with it. Why do you want a colon anyway?
Abel: I've noticed a lot of colons in titles. People seem to use a colon to
           introduce a sort of subheading. *[He pulls a journal from his*

bag.] Here's one from the *British Journal for the Philosophy of Science*. 'Structure: its shadow and substance'. So it's like an announcement, then an explanation. It seems appropriate for what Kim's trying to do.

Barbara: That's a style thing. We're just looking for anything that's obviously wrong. Like commas. She's still putting them in the wrong place and it interrupts the flow of the sentence. Listen: 'Vibrations in machines, platforms and other structures *[she pauses]* cause extra stress and energy loss.' She doesn't need a comma after 'structures' – why has she put one in?

Abel: I agree with you. It doesn't make sense to separate the subject and the verb with a comma.

Barbara: Mmm. Useful rule. *[She writes it down.]* She's probably done it because it's a compound subject and it does make sense to have a comma after 'machines'. But that's all she needs.

Abel: Here's a colon I want to take out. 'A position of stable equilibrium, colon, restoring forces will return the system to this position.' I think she's trying to give an explanation after the colon, but it needs to be introduced by a complete sentence.

Barbara: Let's see? Yes, I think she should just say: 'Restoring forces will return the system to a position of stable equilibrium.' Either that or 'A position of stable equilibrium is required, colon, restoring forces etc.' It's making my head spin.

Abel: So what's the rule? If you're using a colon as a sort of introduction to an explanation, then there has to be a complete sentence before it.

Barbara: Yeah – I'll write that down too. You seem to be obsessed with colons today, Abel.

Abel: Well, my own's not feeling too good. Barbara, I'm going to have to quit. I'd a greasy meal late last night, then another argument with Gus – a really bad one. I'll have to leave you to it, I'm afraid.

Abel returns home, much to Barbara's annoyance as they have all sorts of arrangements for Kim's party to finalize. She continues with her proofreading and decides that the list of rules she has started is a useful one, so she keeps going. When Kim triumphantly finishes writing her speech at 1.30 am, she comes into the kitchen and finds Barbara fast asleep, slumped over the dissertation, with a list of suggestions and a separate list of rules ('don'ts') for punctuation by her side.

10.6.1 Some useful 'don'ts' for punctuation

These are based on the most common errors that students make. (Kim seems to be a typical student!)

- Don't separate a subject and verb with a comma.
- Don't use a comma to separate complete sentences.
- Don't use a comma unless it helps the reader's understanding.
- Don't use a colon to introduce an explanation unless there is a main clause before it.
- Don't use a colon to introduce a list that completes the sentence (e.g. We are learning grammar, language and punctuation.).
- Don't use a semicolon to introduce a list; use a colon instead.
- Don't use quotation marks too often to replace 'so-called': both read like sneering!

If all this seems like a lot to remember, then don't try to. Don't let worrying about punctuation slow your writing down; you can always correct it later. If you know that you have a tendency to make a mistake in one particular area – such as using commas instead of full stops – then do a special proofread looking just for this.

Apart from apostrophes, commas are the most frequently misused punctuation marks. They are likely to have too much work to do, be in the wrong place, or be missing when they are needed for sense.

Many students avoid colons and semicolons altogether because they do not know how to use them. Some famous writers have also avoided them for a variety of reasons (see Truss (2003) for some examples). I agree with Lynne Truss that these punctuation marks are graceful, helping authors to write with style. And often punctuation is just a matter of personal style. If you're scared to use colons and semicolons, then they can be avoided by careful writing. But it is still worth knowing what their functions are.

10.7 Comments on questions

10.7.1 Do you think the sentence in Eddie's letter is more offensive with or without commas? Why?

This is the same point that was made in Chapter 9 about whether a clause defines or describes a noun. In Eddie's version, he is making a statement that describes English fans. This assumes that all English fans get drunk and fight. If you remove the commas, then he is specifying which fans should be ashamed of themselves.

10.7.2 This question relates to the joke behind the title of Lynne Truss's book

What are the main differences between the two pandas:

(a) The panda eats shoots and leaves.
(b) The panda eats, shoots and leaves.

The first panda behaves very typically and the compound object of the sentence is 'shoots and leaves'.

The second panda does three things; this is a compound sentence with three verbs. (One subject covers them all.)

The comma changes the intonation of the sentence as well as the meaning.

10.7.3 If you look for other punctuation jokes on the World Wide Web, the main one you find is a version of the following. A professor asked a class of students to punctuate this sentence.

Woman without her man is nothing

(a) How did the boys punctuate it?
Woman – without her man – is nothing.
(b) How did the girls punctuate it?
Woman – without her, man is nothing.

(There are various alternative possibilities.)

10.7.4 Punctuate the following sentences so that any ambiguity – which may even be offensive – is removed. In most cases, you'll have to put in punctuation but you may need to take some out as well.

(a) Abel laughed and joked about failure an hour after Barbara failed her exam
Abel laughed and joked about failure. An hour after, Barbara failed her exam.
This makes the timing of his laughing clearer. Knowing Abel, he probably still felt bad about it though!

(b) What a mess you have made a difference already though
What a mess! You have made a difference already though.
So we know it's not you that made the mess!

(c) I've got a friend who could ask for anything more
I've got a friend. Who could ask for anything more?
Not a greedy friend who keeps asking for things!

(d) When Kim plays the piano sounds out of tune
When Kim plays, the piano sounds out of tune.
The piano needs tuning. It's not that Kim's a bad player (though she's better on the saxophone).

(e) I'll give Kim, a bag, a box of chocolates and a birthday card
I'll give Kim a bag, a box of chocolates and a birthday card.
Kim might not like being described as a bag!

(f) Kims birthday presents are the following a DVD of the *Rocky Horror Show* the theme for her party cakes, iced with her teams colours to improve her punctuation; a book and a comic recording *Phonetically Speaking* by Victor Borge a bedroom scene a painting she likes chocolates and a bag to hide other unwanted presents

Kim's birthday presents are the following: a DVD of the *Rocky Horror Show* – the theme for her party; cakes, iced with her team's colours; to improve her punctuation, a book and a comic recording (*Phonetically Speaking* by Victor Borge); a bedroom scene (a painting she likes); chocolates; and a bag to hide other, unwanted, presents.

If you're making comments within a list, it's important to know what goes together. Kim wants these presents so the commas round 'unwanted' make a huge difference here.

(g) Isnt that touching Barbara said Abel have you seen the bloke you used to go out with his friend is Kims brother Welsh friends are here too it seems we've got plenty of men if youre looking for someone new Im not the one I want already knows who she is dont you

'Isn't that touching, Barbara?' said Abel. 'Have you seen the bloke you used to go out with? His friend is Kim's brother. Welsh friends are here too. It seems we've got plenty of men, if you're looking for someone new. I'm not. The one I want already knows who she is . . . don't you?'

There are various ways you might punctuate this. You need to know whether Barbara or Abel is the one who is talking. This could also tell you whether Abel is gay or not. I have put an ellipsis (. . .) before the last question to suggest that there is something unspoken here. It is possible to use punctuation to create an impression, though you probably won't do this much in academic writing.

This is the punctuated version of the paragraph in Section 10.3.

There are, I suppose, only a few works that seem even more essential to the Western Canon than *Paradise Lost* – Shakespeare's major tragedies, Chaucer's *Canterbury Tales*, Dante's *Divine Comedy*, the Torah, the Gospels, Cervantes' *Don Quixote*, Homer's epics. Except perhaps for Dante's poem, none of these is as embattled as Milton's dark work. Shakespeare undoubtedly received provocation from rival playwrights, while Chaucer charmingly cited fictive authorities and concealed his authentic obligations to Dante and Boccaccio. The Hebrew Bible and the Greek New Testament were revised into their present forms by redactionists who may have shared very little with the original authors whom they were editing. Cervantes, with unsurpassed mirth, parodied unto death his chivalric forerunners, while we do not have the texts of Homer's precursors.

(Bloom 1994: 26)

10.8 Conclusion: advice about punctuation

If you're getting confused over punctuation, it may be that you are still sorting out the ideas that you want to write about. It's a good idea to get your ideas down and then worry about the punctuation later. Here are some tips to help you when you are reading over your own work:

- Use punctuation to help you to complete sentences and alert readers to appropriate groupings of words within them.
- Think about whether you are completing, introducing, separating, enclosing or omitting.
- Read your work aloud to help you to hear the rhythms of your sentences.
- Ask someone else to proofread your work and tell you when they are puzzled about something you have written. It may be that the punctuation is not helping the meaning.
- Make a special check for punctuation that you know you often get wrong.

10.8.1 Technical terms relating to this chapter

For further information, look up these words in the Glossary, other grammar books or the World Wide Web.

Bracket
Colon
Comma
Dash
Hyphen
Ellipsis
Full stop
Inverted comma
Parenthesis
Period
Question mark
Quotation mark
Scare quotes
Semicolon

11

That pesky apostrophe

11.1 Getting possessive and going missing • 11.2 Questions about apostrophes • 11.3 What's happening to the apostrophe? • 11.4 How to use an apostrophe to show possession • 11.5 How to use an apostrophe to show omission • 11.6 Hold the apostrophe! • 11.7 That Lynne Truss has a lot to answer for! • 11.8 Comments on questions • 11.9 Conclusion: advice about apostrophes

We have reached number 1 in lecturers' pet hates: misuse of the apostrophe.

11.1 Getting possessive and going missing

Kim looks at the note that Barbara has left her and snorts (see Figure 11.1 on page 122). She doesn't notice Barbara coming back into the kitchen.

Kim: Why are my friends odd? And which brother's pal?
Barbara: Fifty-odd friends. Perhaps you should reduce that by one: you sounded sneery about me there. And I think Calum is a friend of both Eddie and Derek, from the way he was talking, anyway. Posh bloke.
Kim: Oh, Barbara – sorry. I didn't see you. I've been waiting for two calls, actually. Calum is Eddie's and Derek's friend but Joe is just Eddie's friend; Derek can't stand him. And I can't stand Calum!

Barbara: Oh, happy families again.

Kim: Actually, if it was Calum who rang, your note should have the apostrophe after the s, because he's the friend of my two brothers. My brothers' (apostrophe) friend.

Barbara: Since when did you become an expert on the apostrophe?

Kim: Since I finished this book. *[She shows Barbara **Eats, Shoots and Leaves** by Lynne Truss.]*

Barbara: Did Abel give you that for your birthday? We were going to get you that and other stuff together. Wait till I see 'im. He's very possessive about that book; insisted on getting it himself for you. But I didn't think he'd give you it yet.

Kim: I'm not bothered who gets what. And you don't need to get me anything – really. It's not necessary. No need for a lovers' tiff.

Barbara: I don't know where you get this idea from Kim. I like Abel but I'm not sure . . . actually I heard a rumour that worried me a bit.

Kim: Eddie's got plans for you anyway. I think Calum's his little surprise for you. He's an expert on grammar, but he's always sneering at people who can't afford to go to posh schools. His was known for its grammar, but it's not made his manners any better. I think Eddie thinks you'll fancy him. Maybe that'll make Abel jealous.

Barbara: Your brother's a pest! Your brother Eddie, anyway.

Kim: Now, now – he's OK. He's got his faults, but haven't we all? I'm the only one allowed to criticize him. *[Looks at watch.]* Oh, it's one o'clock – goin' crazy – must dash.

Barbara: And why should I fancy Calum if he sneers at people?

Kim: You'll need to learn some put-downs for people who sneer. Our grammar's getting pretty good and we've done it all ourselves – we didn't have his advantages. Thanks for the proofreading, by the way – you missed a few things but you did pick up things that I didn't. Now, go and make up with Abel and take him some grapes. And you'll need to shift some of this furniture if we've got so many people coming. I'll be out for the rest of the day.

Barbara: But . . .

Kim: And Abel didn't give me the book; I got it at Christmas. But something's clicked and I understand it properly now.

But Kim is already disappearing out the door as she says this and Barbara doesn't hear her. Barbara has so much more to think about anyway.

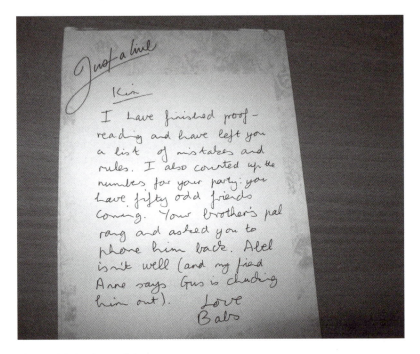

Figure 11.1   An ambiguous note

11.2 Questions about apostrophes

1 In the passage above, what comments might you make about punctuation (or lack of it) in the following expressions:

(a) And which brother's pal?
(b) He's the friend of my two brothers
(c) My brothers' . . . friend
(d) Wait till I see 'im.
(e) It's not necessary
(f) a lovers' tiff
(g) His was known for its grammar, but it's not made his manners any better.
(h) your brother's a pest
(i) it's one o'clock – goin' crazy
(j) Our grammar's getting pretty good

2 Do you think that we should abolish the apostrophe?

3 Should we write St James Park, St Jame's Park, St James' Park or St James's Park?

There are comments on these questions in Section 11.8.

11.3 What's happening to the apostrophe?

There are many debates about the apostrophe. As we saw in Chapter 1, its misuse is lecturers' number 1 hate, but nowadays some lecturers don't know how to use it properly either. Some experts think that the apostrophe has had its day and that it would be better to get rid of it altogether. If it doesn't aid understanding, then what is the point of it?

Other writers – including me – would like to see the apostrophe restored to its proper use. It does help to avoid confusion; as the following examples show, the apostrophe is sometimes actually necessary to know what is happening.

> The authors' work has contributed to government policy.
> The bands' music made T in the Park a success.

Here we know – because of the position of the apostrophe – that more than one author or band was involved. If this is not acknowledged, then perhaps only the last mentioned author or band gets the credit and the others get offended.

I was recently involved in an exchange on a discussion board that showed how important the apostrophe can be.

> *James:* I'd like to thank Christine for doing this.
> *Mary:* Can I add my thanks to James?
> *James:* No, it was Christine who did it.

But Mary knew that anyway! If Mary had written, 'Can I add my thanks to James'?' then it would have been clearer. If she had used the style James's, that would perhaps have been clearer still. (Either would be acceptable.)

A possible problem with the apostrophe is that its uses create other associations.

It is associated with possession – belonging to something. However, this doesn't apply to *possessive adjectives* and *possessive pronouns*.

> The student's book.   BUT   Your book. It is yours.
>   His book. It is his.
>   Her book. It is hers.

It is used for abbreviating words, but then they can sound like other words (especially certain kinds of adjective).

You're a star.   BUT   Your star is in its ascendancy.
They're working. BUT   Their work is important.
It's beautiful.   BUT   You are the reason for its beauty.

There are some tricky examples of usage.

Women's work   'Women' is already a plural
Dickens's novels   'Dickens' novels' would also be acceptable
Mind your p's and q's   The apostrophe helps the reader to see what is
                                       intended

Many writers are aware that there are some awkward aspects to apostrophes, but don't know how to get round them. They then just tend to shove one in whenever there is an s or never use them at all.

11.4 How to use an apostrophe to show possession

Even though there are many public examples of missing or misused apostrophes, it is still an advantage to know how to use them. You will please many of your tutors and professors; you will impress employers and other professional contacts. Figure 11.2 is a reminder for how to use it to show possession; keep it by your side when you're checking over an essay or report before handing it in.

When possession is being shown, there are two nouns together. The second one is possessed by the first. Figure 11.2 should help you to see the patterns of when this should come before or after a final s.

Either Dickens' novels or Dickens's novels would be correct. St James' Park is in Newcastle and St James's Park is in London. What does this tell us? Well, it shows that there is more than one accepted approach to this – but a Google search led me to discover that feelings can run quite high in favour of either or none at all! And there is precedent for none at all. St Albans and St Andrews are both places that have managed very well without an apostrophe.

It does make it more difficult for students when there is disagreement over these issues. Some people contributing to the debate make very strong claims about the poor education of people who took the other side, demonstrating in the process the kind of sneering that this book is trying to avoid. It is awkward, as convincing cases can be made for any of the positions. In such cases, I would usually take the line that upsets the fewest people – or rewrite the sentence to avoid it if I can.

Apostrophe *before* the s

if you want to show that a singular noun is possessive (owns something)

Kim's brother	the brother of Kim
the apostrophe's use	the use of the apostrophe

if you want to show that an indefinite pronoun is possessive

nobody's child	the child of nobody
if one's husband is the duke	the husband of one

if you want to show that a plural noun that does not end in s is possessive

children's playground	the playground of the children
the men's room	the room of the men
the women's rooms	the rooms of the women
people's rights	the rights of the people

Apostrophe *after* the s

if you want to show that a plural noun ending in s is possessive

the brothers' homes	the homes of the brothers
the apostrophes' uses	the uses of the apostrophes
three weeks' time	the time of three weeks
MPs' votes	the votes of MPs

If you want to show that a singular noun that ends in s is possessive

for goodness' sake	for the sake of goodness
for Jesus' sake	for the sake of Jesus
Dickens' novels	the novels of Dickens

Figure 11.2   Using an apostrophe to show possession

11.5 How to use an apostrophe to show omission

The other use of the apostrophe is to indicate missing letters, in abbreviated forms or in conventional uses where letters are missing.

11.5.1 Abbreviating part of the verb 'to be' or 'to have'

It is recommended that you avoid the abbreviations below in academic writing; they are not usually appropriate. In particular, a useful rule is never use it's in academic writing.

I'm	I am	you're	you are
he's	he is/has	Kim's	Kim is/has
it's	it is/has	we're	we are
they're	they are	I'll	I will/shall
I'd	I had	I've	I have

11.5.2 Abbreviating 'not'

Again, you would not usually see the following in academic writing, but this is a correct use of the apostrophe: won't, shan't, don't, didn't, wouldn't, shouldn't.

11.5.3 Showing there is a missing letter or group of letters

The most common example is o'clock (of the clock), and this is a use that you might see in academic writing. It is sometimes used to show abbreviated dates: Christmas '99, June '09. It is not, however, necessary when talking about groups of years:

Remember the 1960s? '68 was especially exciting.

An apostrophe is often used to show how people speak, particularly a dropped h or a dropped g. For example, I'll kill 'im, goin' crazy. If it is important for you to capture exactly how someone talks, then you might use apostrophes in this way.

11.6 Hold the apostrophe!

A famous sneer about apostrophes is the expression 'the *greengrocer's apostrophe*'. This refers to the habit of some shopkeepers to add an apostrophe before any s. So outside a greengrocer's, there might be a sign saying: 'Carrot's, apple's, potatoe's'. Such signs were often to be seen on windows of shops or on market stalls.

It's a sign of the times (or perhaps some of my personal habits) that I became more aware of this with chip shops. I used to work next to a busy shop in the centre of Glasgow that sold a variety of foods at lunchtime and frequently put up adverts, sometimes painted on the windows, to announce this. As well as pie's, chip's, roll's etc., I noticed one day that they promised 'deliciou's snack's'. The signwriter seemed to have a rule that if there is an s at the end of a word, it needs an apostrophe before it.

I saw a nice example in my local coffee shop, Joanna Goodbite, where they seemed to be using an apostrophe as a sort of crouton. A lecturer in the queue ahead of me said it was very confusing for his students to be told off for this kind of thing only to get it with their lunch! They kindly let me take a photo in return for a copy of this book: see Figure 11.3.

Figure 11.3   An apostrophe in the soup

When I ask students what is wrong with such signs, they can always tell me. But then they make similar mistakes themselves. I have on occasion used the 'chip shop apostrophe' myself – though I usually manage to catch it before anyone sees it. I probably miss it sometimes, though; I have seen it done by people who definitely know better but have written an email or a note in a hurry. I think what happens is that people 'hear' an apostrophe before an s in their head as they are writing and the wrong version gets written down. This is why checking your work is so important.

An s at the end of the word, then, is a trigger for people to think 'should there be an apostrophe here or not?' Until you are on top of the uses of the apostrophe as shown in Figure 11.2, you won't want to stop yourself at the end of every word ending in s – you'd never get anything written! But it's something to bear in mind when you're checking your work over.

Just to reinforce the point, do NOT use an apostrophe for:

simple plurals	The sources consulted were academic books and journals, the public records and the local newspapers.
its (unless it is short for 'it is' or 'it has')	The company is proud of its achievements.
possessive pronouns	Your books are overdue; if it is a problem, it is theirs.

The greengrocer's apostrophe – where a simple plural is turned into a singular *possessive* – is probably the main cause of distress for the many people who would like punctuation to be used properly. It is so public that it encourages even more wrong use. This upset some people so much that they set up an *Apostrophe Protection Society*. You can see their website at www.apostrophe.org.uk.

By the way, you should read Lynne Truss's book if you want to know why we shouldn't sneer at greengrocers.

11.7 That Lynne Truss has a lot to answer for!

Why did the Apostrophe Protection Society not have a militant wing? Could I start one? Where do you get balaclavas?

(Truss 2003: 4)

Things aren't going too well for our students at the moment. Barbara is annoyed with Abel because she thinks he's given Kim their present in advance. She's also heard that he's in a spot of trouble. She doesn't know how reliable this is, but it's making her wonder if she really knows him. She also doesn't like the sound of Calum, though part of her is interested by the attention she's getting. Her essay marks have improved considerably, though for the first time she has failed a small exam and that's making her wonder if she's managing her time properly. Abel is still feeling queasy; he's worried about Gus, money and his laptop. Something else is also niggling him; he has a sense of something looming. Kim is overdoing everything. Derek saw her disappearing round the corner with a large cardboard apostrophe on a stick and a pot of white paint.

Barbara and Derek are sharing a beer in Kim's kitchen.

Barbara: So what's your friend Calum like then?

Derek: Hard to describe. He's taking the mickey most of the time, so you shouldn't take any notice of him. He's OK. Make sure you know what a subjunctive is, though.

Barbara: Oh, so he's sneery. The grammar pals don't like sneering. At least, I thought we didn't. Kim's getting odd about punctuation. It's as if a light's gone on. A week ago, she didn't know anything about commas and apostrophes and that – now she does.

Derek: I don't think she's sneering – it's much worse than that. She's militant!

Barbara: What do you mean?

Derek: Well, I think she's gone out to 'correct' the posters on that shop round the corner.

Barbara: You're joking. She'll get caught.

Derek: She was always passionate about things. Even as a wee kid. We were always rescuing her from fights and arguments.

Abel arrives, with a copy of *Eats, Shoots and Leaves* and a CD.

Barbara: Abel, what were you doing giving Kim her present in advance? It's made her go doo-lally. We agreed that we'd do something together. You really get on my nerves sometimes.

Abel: What are you talking about? I've got part of her present here. Did you get the chocolates and the bag? Here's the book you said to get. And a CD I found. Victor Borge.

Barbara: Oh, I'm sorry. I thought you must have given her it. Well, she's got the book already then. We'll have to get something else.

Abel: Barbara, I can't afford anything else. I'm skint, remember. We've got enough here – if you've got your bits that is. This CD's got a

> track called 'Phonetic Punctuation' – it's dead funny. But don't ask
> me to spend any more.

Barbara: Well, there might not be a party anyway. Kim seems to have other
plans. She's gone out to attack people with an apostrophe on a stick.

Derek: I think we need to go and find her. Come on, Barbara.

But when they get to the shop round the corner, it's already too late. Kim is
outside the shop, painting out the apostrophes on the notices about chip's and
pie's on the window. She doesn't need her apostrophe on a stick; there are
extra apostrophes everywhere. But she's noticed that there's one missing in
the nearby travel agent's and she plans to move on there later, to stand in front
of the sign that says: 'Your journeys end – paradise' holding the apostrophe
between journey and s. When the others get to her, it's just in time to hear the
shop owner shouting: 'And I've called the police.'

11.8 Comments on questions

11.8.1 In the passage above, what comments might you make about punctuation (or lack of it) in the following expressions:

(a) **And which brother's pal?**
This apostrophe is used for possession and refers to one brother. An
apostrophe after the s might also be acceptable, as Kim has so many
brothers.

(b) **He's the friend of my two brothers**
The apostrophe here shows a missing letter; this is short for 'He is . . .'.

(c) **My brothers' . . . friend**
There is definitely more than one brother involved.

(d) **Wait till I see 'im.**
Missing letter – Barbara's dropping her aitches.

(e) **It's not necessary**
The apostrophe shows that an i is missing. It is not necessary.

(f) **a lovers' tiff**
Here, more than one lover is involved. If I had used the apostrophe before
the s, it would suggest that only one was in fighting mood.

(g) **His was known for its grammar, but it's not made his manners
any better.**
When it's has an apostrophe, it can be short for it is or it has. Without an
apostrophe, it shows possession (like his).

(h) **your brother's a pest**
Your doesn't need an apostrophe – and the apostrophe in brother's

is not possession this time; it shows a missing letter. Your brother is a pest.

(i) **it's one o'clock – goin' crazy**
More missing letters – of the clock; going crazy. Kim likes music and 'Goin' crazy' is a song title, so she might be dropping the g because she's thinking of this.

(j) **Our grammar's getting pretty good**
Our grammar is getting pretty good.

11.8.2 Do you think that we should abolish the apostrophe?

Obviously, there is no 'correct' answer to this question – I just wanted you to ask it of yourself. There are certainly strong feelings about it. It seems a shame that something that should be useful is not, because it is so indiscriminately used. I personally think that I'd prefer it to disappear than keep getting used unhelpfully, but on the whole I hope we can keep it.

11.8.3 Should we write St James Park, St Jame's Park, St James' Park or St James's Park?

You would be OK with any except the second, though it would depend on your reference. It may be necessary to refer to an atlas if you want to make sure you are correct.

11.9 Conclusion: advice about apostrophes

- Never abbreviate 'it's' in formal writing – write 'it is' instead.
- Apostrophes are not used with possessive adjectives: my, your, her, his, its, our, their.
- Apostrophes are not used with possessives without nouns: mine, yours, hers, his, ours, theirs.
- Apostrophes are not used with simple plurals.
- They are not necessary with groups of years, e.g. 1960s.
- When you use an apostrophe to show ownership, the apostrophe goes after the owner.
- Place names can be tricky and it's best to check an atlas.

| The woman's book | owner = the woman |
| The women's room | owner = the women |

11.9.1 Technical terms relating to this chapter

For further information, look up these words in the Glossary, other grammar books or the World Wide Web.

Abbreviation
Apostrophe
Apostrophe Protection Society
Genitive case
Greengrocer's apostrophe
Indefinite pronoun
Possessive adjective
Possessive pronoun

12

Checking the checker

Once we know how to do things, human beings like to automate them so we don't have to worry about them. Automation helps to extend human abilities by allowing us to do more. Undoubtedly, this makes life a lot easier. We can calculate a lot of numbers very quickly with calculators and spreadsheets. We can check our spelling and grammar using spelling and grammar checkers. But if we don't understand what the calculator or checker is telling us, then we're not extending our abilities. We are taking a gamble that the technology will do our work for us.

The main message of this chapter is that the grammar checker should work with you rather than for you.

12.1 A house of correction

Unfortunately, Kim has been arrested for defacing property (though she insists that she was un-defacing it). This is not good news; she is due to give a formal presentation to industrial sponsors the next day and her party is the day after that.

Her friends and brothers are worried that in her excitement she'll make the situation worse. They decide to write a letter to the police explaining the circumstances and take it down to the station later. This is their first draft, typed by Derek in a bit of a hurry.

> Dear Sir or Madam
> We are written to request leniency in the case of our sister and friend Kim. The removal of apostrophes which she done today were because of her passion for good punctuation. She as been working very hard on her dissertation for university and has a important presentation to do tomorrow. We can ensure you that we wont be letting her do this anymore. Her behavior will be appropriate from now on.
> Yours

Barbara is exasperated as she reads over Derek's shoulder.

Barbara: Derek – that's full of mistakes. They'll think we're a bunch of illiterates!
Abel: Barbara! Sneering!
Derek: What does the checker say? Look – there are two squiggly green lines. That means something's wrong. It doesn't like 'apostrophes which' and it doesn't like 'a important'. Oh yes, that should be 'an'.
Barbara: And there's nothing wrong with 'apostrophes which'.
Abel: But there is something wrong with 'which she done'.
Derek: I'll run the checker properly and see what it says. Look, it wants to put a comma after which. I'll just go OK – change.
Barbara: No – you don't need to . . . Oh, now what is it saying?
Derek: Incomplete thought. Right – it wants a verb. So you grammar experts can tell me what verb it wants. What's a verb anyway?
Barbara: Start again. This is a mess.

They muddle through and it still doesn't look right. But when they run the checker again it says: 'The grammar check is complete'.

Abel: Try it at a higher setting – a formal setting.
Derek: *[Changes the setting]* Now it says the first sentence is passive.
Barbara: And I'm not. Or I won't be for much longer.

12.2 Questions about grammar checkers

1 Here is the students' letter again. Can you find all the mistakes? If you can be bothered, you might like to type it out and run it through your own grammar checker to see whether it agrees with you.

> Dear Sir or Madam
>   We are written to request leniency in the case of our sister and friend Kim. The removal of apostrophes which she done today were because of her passion for good punctuation. She as been working very hard on her dissertation for university and has a important presentation to do tomorrow. We can ensure you that we wont be letting her do this anymore. Her behaviour will be appropriate from now on.

2 Look back over the topics in this book (for example, look at the Contents page). Which do you think would give the grammar checker the most difficulty?

There are comments on these questions in Section 12.6.

12.3 Pitfalls with grammar checkers

Grammar checkers are getting more sophisticated but they still can't tell exactly what you're trying to say. Many students trust them because they are so unsure of their own grammar; they assume that the checker must be right. I often hear students say, 'The grammar checker put a comma there.' But unfortunately, lecturers will hold you rather than the grammar checker responsible for wrong spelling and grammar.

    There are various possible pitfalls:

- The checker does not recognize that something is correct.
- The checker does not recognize that something is incorrect.
- The setting is inappropriate; a common example is using a US dictionary for work in the UK, resulting in spellings such as 'flavor' instead of 'flavour'.
- The checker can't distinguish between some frequently confused words.
- You can't understand what the checker is telling you.
- If there are a lot of errors, the grammar checker has difficulty in recognizing some of them until others are corrected.
- Once you have pressed 'Change' or 'Ignore' then the checker will accept it, even if you run it again.
- It is possible to 'teach' the checker to approve of your mistakes – for example, by putting a misspelling into its dictionary.

- If you deliberately want to write something that is technically wrong, then you have to be careful that the checker doesn't change it. This is a problem for writing a book like this, for example. If I want to say that students frequently tell me they are having problems with their 'grammer', I don't want the checker to change this wrong use or my point will be missed!

Figure 12.1 shows another example of a passage that shows some of the pitfalls. It is an exercise that I sometimes use with students as a demonstration of how checkers can be both useful and not useful at once. In Figure 12.2, I show what my own grammar checker made of each sentence.

Your friend has asked you to proofread an essay. Identify spelling mistakes and grammar errors in the paragraphs below, and then compare it with the advice from the grammar checker. NB: there are some mistakes on this page that the Word grammar checker has not picked up.

Studying language

Students must learn to write in the language of there subject area, this is because they are 'trying on' the discourse of that subject. But how are they expected to do this if they have never encountered any writing in this style before. Coming from school or college which means that they have more or less been told what to write. At University it is very different, you have to do your own work and be comitted to finding things out for oneself. If you have wrote something in the wrong style, the lecturers will give you feedback but some writers say that the style should be taught along with the subject mater. Even more than that, errors in grammar occurs because of the complexity of the ideas and not because the student always gets it wrong . Nightingale (1988) suggests that trying to improve grammar without taking context into account is a waste of time. Context is described by some writers as more than just background; it is also an integral part of the practice.

Students are joining new community's of practice and have to learn how they operate. It is wrong from lecturers' to say that there grammar should of been corrected at school, it is up to the lecturers to help them in this new context.

Reference

Nightingale, P. (1988) Language and learning: a bibliographical essay, in G. Taylor, B. Ballard, V. Beasley, H. Bock, J. Clanchy and P. Nightingale (eds), *Literacy by Degrees*. Milton Keynes: SRHE and Open University Press.

Figure 12.1   A passage to put through a grammar checker

Sentence	What one grammar checker found (and missed)
Students must learn to write in the language of there subject area, this is because they are 'trying on' the discourse of that subject.	It picked up the wrong spelling of 'their' but missed the run-on sentence.
But how are they expected to do this if they have never encountered any writing in this style before.	It didn't like me starting a sentence with 'But' and suggested 'However', which would probably be better for formal writing. If I didn't accept this change, then it missed that this was a question.
Coming from school or college which means that they have more or less been told what to write.	It suggested using a comma after 'college' (correct) or change 'which' to 'that' – so I had to make a choice. It did recognize that this was an incomplete sentence and didn't like the passive.
At University it is very different, you have to do your own work and be comitted to finding things out for oneself.	It picked up the misspelling (committed) but missed the fact that this was a run-on sentence. It wanted a comma after University. It missed the mis-relationship between 'you' and 'oneself'.
If you have wrote something in the wrong style, the lecturers will give you feedback but some writers say that the style should be taught along with the subject mater.	It didn't like the passive construction, but missed the wrong past participle (wrote) and misspelling of 'matter'. ('Mater' is an actual word.)
Even more than that, errors in grammar occurs because of the complexity of the ideas and not because the student always gets it wrong .	It spotted the extra space before the full stop. (This can be very useful.) It missed the mix of singular and plural in 'errors … occurs'.
Nightingale (1988) suggests that trying to improve grammar without taking context into account is a waste of time.	It suggested 'taking context into account' was too wordy and should be replaced by 'considering context' (good idea).
Context is described by some writers as more than just background; it is also an integral part of the practice.	It didn't like the passive and offered a better suggestion: Some writers describe context.
Students are joining new community's of practice and have to learn how they operate.	It suggested, correctly, replacing 'community's' with 'communities'.
It is wrong from lecturers' to say that there grammar should of been corrected at school, it is up to the lecturers to help them in this new context.	It picked up the wrong use of 'of' instead of 'have'. It missed the wrong *preposition* in 'It is wrong from'. It missed the unnecessary apostrophe. It only picked up the wrong 'there' if I corrected the run-on sentence as it suggested, by using a semicolon.

Figure 12.2 What a grammar checker found and missed

12.4 How to use a grammar checker knowledgeably

Barbara decides to have another shot at writing a letter to the police. She doesn't want to hurt Derek's feelings, but thinks that his effort is unlikely to impress them. As they are using excellence in punctuation as their plea, the letter has to be correct. Here is her attempt.

Dear Sir or Madam

Earlier today Kim W—— was arrested for defacing property at a shop on the corner of Argyle Street.

We are a group of students who have been learning about grammar and Kim had been upset about the misues of the apostrophe in the shop. She was editing, she wanted to make the display easier to understand.

Kim has been overworking lately and has a great deal on her mind, including a presentation that she has to make tomorrow (Friday). We wish to make a plea for her release and promise to ensure that she does not cause any further distress.

Yours faithfully

The grammar checker puts a green squiggle under 'was arrested' and a red one under 'misues'.

Barbara: Was arrested – passive. That's OK. I don't particularly want to draw attention to who arrested her! And misues – typing error. I'll correct that. Is there anything else? What about 'who have been learning'? It hasn't marked that. No, it's OK – no commas needed. It's let the comma after 'editing' go, but I think that should really be a semicolon because there are two complete sentences here.

That is the kind of conversation you should have with yourself when you use the grammar checker.

Figure 12.2 shows how a checker can be very helpful, offering useful suggestions for improvement. It also shows that it can miss things or offer inappropriate alternatives because it is unaware of your context. It is important to be able to interpret its messages.

12.5 What happens next?

Barbara takes the letter to the police station, while Derek and Abel go to the shop to see if they can reason with the owner. The owner's son is there, discussing the incident with his dad, and laughing about it. He thinks that Kim has made an improvement and that they should also make a little story about it for the local press. It would be good publicity for the shop. When Derek and Abel say why they have come, the father looks a bit fierce but the son is friendly.

Owner's son:	I'll do a short press release about this. I'm supposed to do one for an assignment – I'm doing media studies at the uni.
Abel:	I'm at the uni too – and so's Kim, the person who was arrested. Er – you wouldn't want to see a fellow student in trouble, would you?
Owner's son:	Depends on the student. I'd have some arrested like a shot. And some lecturers.
Derek:	Oh no, I think you'd like Kim. She's great fun. And she'll invite you to her party if you help her out. It's a Rocky Horror Show party.
Owner's son:	Oh, that party – I've heard about that. Wouldn't mind going to it actually.

They all go to the police station where Barbara is at the counter trying to get attention. She is horrified when she sees who is with them.

Barbara:	Mark, what are you doing here?

It turns out that the shop owner's son is the guy, Mark, who went out with Barbara the previous semester (and who has been the cause of a great deal of her moaning about men).
    A little later . . .

Derek:	You lot – you just can't escape punctuation!
Barbara:	What do you mean?
Derek:	Well, the police are going to question Mark.
Barbara:	Doh! That's *so* not funny.

12.6 Comments on questions

12.6.1 Here is the students' letter again. Can you find all the mistakes? If you can be bothered, you might like to type it out and run it through your own grammar checker to see whether it agrees with you.

Dear Sir or Madam

We are ~~written~~ writing to request leniency in the case of our sister and friend Kim. The removal of apostrophes which she ~~done~~ did today ~~were~~ was because of her passion for good punctuation. She has been working very hard on her dissertation for university and has an important presentation to do tomorrow. We can ~~ensure~~ assure you that we won't be letting her do this anymore. Her behaviour will be appropriate from now on.

12.6.2 Look back over the topics in this book (for example, look at the Contents page). Which do you think would give the grammar checker the most difficulty?

Here are some suggestions.

Chapter 2	The grammar checker can't distinguish between easily confused words, though it sometimes will point out when they arise. Often, though, that makes students change a correct word to a wrong one! You may have to put frequently used technical words into its dictionary.
Chapter 3	Grammar checkers are of course trying to ensure that we conform to standard practice, but there can still be problems when the writing is sophisticated. Checkers can be set for different levels so that they can distinguish between Standard English and less formal writing.
Chapter 4	When there are compound subjects it may be difficult for the checker to recognize this.
Chapter 5	There are so many possible uses for words ending in -ing or -ed that it might offer the wrong suggestions. It certainly will look for verbs – and try to ensure that they are complete (finite).
Chapter 6	Grammar checkers are usually quite good at recognizing sentences but not always.
Chapter 7	You may see references to comma splices or sentence fragments. Checkers are quite helpful here and getting better. It is always worth rereading anything that a checker is highlighting; but you need to make the decision yourself.
Chapter 8	Checkers often recommend active verbs rather than passive,

	though you can change this if you want. Reflective writing might need to be assessed at a different level.
Chapter 9	Checkers are fussy about 'that' and 'which', as we saw in Chapter 9. They may be unnecessarily so.
Chapter 10	The checker will not always recognize when punctuation is ambiguous.
Chapter 11	The grammar checker knows that 'your' is frequently confused with 'you're' and may ask if you want to change your version. It does the same with 'it's' and 'its'. Just because it asks if you want to change, it doesn't mean it would be correct to do so!
Chapter 13	We haven't got to this chapter yet. But grammar is significant for both avoidance of plagiarism and for its detection. If someone plagiarizes someone else's bad grammar, the checker might help to pick this up.

12.7 Conclusion: advice about grammar checkers

There is really only one piece of advice about using a grammar checker:

Make sure that you understand what it is telling you.

13

Quote/unquote–avoiding plagiarism

13.1 Credit where it's due • 13.2 Questions about referencing • 13.3 Grammar and punctuation in referencing • 13.4 What goes in the quotation marks? • 13.5 Double or single quotes • 13.6 Different systems for referencing • 13.7 Oh what a giveaway • 13.8 In your own words • 13.9 Comments on questions • 13.10 Conclusion: advice about avoiding plagiarism

While referencing (or citation) practices do not strictly belong to the category of grammar, there is a fair amount of overlap with other issues in this book. Our students are about to discover that grammatical knowledge can be a key not only to referencing properly, but also to exposing plagiarism.

13.1 Credit where it's due

Barbara is wishing she hadn't said quite so much about Mark on Twitter and Facebook. It's only a day since the incident at the police station, but he is already following her on Twitter and is her friend on Facebook so he has access to quite a trail of tweets and status declarations. She is at her computer busy clearing away the evidence from these and other social networking sites when

Abel arrives at the flat with a suitcase. Kim has agreed that Abel can move in; he has had enough of Gus.

Abel: Hi, Barbara – is Kim in?

Barbara: No, she's away to see about references.

Abel: I didn't think I'd need references to move in. She knows me.

Barbara: No, silly, it's not about you. It's about references for her dissertation. She's not sure how to lay it out. Whether it's Harvard or Chicago style, you know. Perhaps some other style.

Abel: No, I don't know. You've lost me.

Barbara: Abel, you must use some kind of referencing system in your essays. Like, you cited that guy with the metaphors – Brian Silver – in your assignment on paradigm shifts.

Abel: Well, yeah. I put the name and year in brackets in the essay when I quoted him. Then I put the details in a list at the end. Didn't do it properly though – I need to figure out how to do that.

Barbara: You certainly do. How did you get through first year? They're so strict about referencing on my modules.

Abel: Well, I was OK with what I was doing in first year – just footnotes. But this new professor wants it differently. He's talking about citation not referencing.

Barbara: I think it's the same thing.

Abel: OK – well, that explains it maybe. I'm glad we did that list of punctuation marks; it's made me realize how much punctuation seems to matter for doing citation.

Barbara: Yes, the different styles use different punctuation. We have to use Harvard.

Abel: Style. The prof said something about APA style. Does that ring any bells?

Barbara: *[Googles 'APA citation']* Here we are. So it looks like author's name and initials, date, title, title of publication and then various other bits. Depending on whether it's a journal article, or a book, or a website.

Abel: And is it a name and date in the essay itself?

Barbara: Yeah – either in parentheses – that's that posh word for round brackets – or as part of the text. I hadn't thought about that – but I suppose there are grammar reasons for whether it's in brackets or not.

Abel: How do you mean?

Barbara: Well, if you're saying 'Silver uses the metaphor of a raft', then Silver is the subject of the sentence. You couldn't really put him in brackets; it wouldn't make sense. So it would just be the year of publication in brackets. But if Silver is just an aside, then his name goes in the brackets too.

Abel: Say that again.

> Barbara is about to explain again, but there is a tweeting noise on her com-
> puter. She reads a short message on her screen, then looks at Abel oddly.
>
> *Barbara:*   You seem to be in trouble, mate. A little bird's just told me.

13.2 Questions about referencing

1 Why do we use *references* in academic writing?
2 Can you name any major *citation styles*?
3 What are the main differences between bibliographic citation and foot-
   noting?
4 What is the difference between direct and indirect citation?
5 Is it plagiarism if you paraphrase or translate someone else's work?
6 How would you make reference to this book?

There are comments on these questions in Section 13.9.

13.3 Grammar and punctuation in referencing

This chapter draws on a number of grammatical points and punctuation marks
that have already been covered in the book. I see many students who have
problems with *referencing conventions*, and it is much easier to explain if they
understand sentences and punctuation.

I often use the metaphor of a conversation or dialogue when I am talking
about academic writing. As a student, you are entering a set of dialogues that
have been going on for a long time in your chosen subjects. To participate, you
need to make references to other people involved in that dialogue.

We reference other writers to acknowledge their ideas. By providing detailed
information on these sources, we give the reader the opportunity to go and
find out more about specific topics. That means that the reader needs to
know exactly who is saying what and where the ideas can be found. A number
of different referencing conventions have developed to make this happen
without interfering too greatly with the reading. It is very important, then,
that referencing fits in with the grammar of the sentence.

As Barbara has pointed out, knowing about grammar and punctuation is an
aid to referencing. It will be helpful to be able to think about the subject of the
sentence. To reference properly, it is especially important that you understand
quotation marks and parentheses. You may also have to use commas, colons,
full stops, square brackets and ellipses in referencing.

To start us off, let's think about the example that Barbara used.

Silver uses the metaphor of a raft.

This simple statement acknowledges Silver's ideas and then allows the writer to go on and comment on the appropriateness of this metaphor. The reader may be interested in Silver and needs to know who Silver is. There are several ways that this might be signalled: here are two of them.

Silver (1998) uses the metaphor of a raft.

Silver[1] uses the metaphor of a raft.

In the first example, the date shows the year of publication, letting the reader know that there is a full reference to this at the end of the piece of writing. In the second example, the superscript 1 shows that there is a footnote or endnote that provides the information.

Notice that the grammar of the sentence might affect how we do this. Here is an alternative way of expressing the idea.

The metaphor of a raft explains the differences between Popper's and Kuhn's positions.

Now I want to acknowledge that this is not my idea, but Brian Silver's. I need to put his name into the sentence, without spoiling the sentence. I can do it as an aside, using parentheses to enclose it.

The metaphor of a raft (Silver 1998) explains the differences between Popper's and Kuhn's positions.

If you look at the books and journals you are using, you will probably see either something in parentheses or a number to alert you to a reference either at the bottom of the page or the end of the piece of writing. You are expected to do something similar when you join in the dialogue.

13.4 What goes in the quotation marks?

Students often want to use someone else's words. 'There seems to be no other way of writing this,' they tell me. I can understand this. Brian Silver writes: 'Working within the paradigm is not necessarily second-class science' (Silver 1998: 105). This is an elegant sentence that could be awkward if I tried to rewrite it. But I do need to be clear why I am using it – for example, I might want to elaborate on the reasons for this and bring in some other authors too. For example:

> Brian Silver writes: 'Working within the paradigm is not necessarily second-class science' (Silver 1998: 105). Silver cites the discovery of DNA as an example of successful working within the paradigm. Indeed, Medawar (1996: 97) points out that Linus Pauling very nearly got there first, before Crick and Watson. The discovery depended on several other pieces of scientific work. Judgements about scientific discovery may therefore relate more to their potential future use than to whether they changed a paradigm.

Notice that I am drawing my own conclusion about the sources I am citing, rather than expecting my readers to do it themselves. Using citations is not a short cut for doing the thinking for yourself.

At the end of the writing, the reference list is in alphabetical order.

> Medawar, P. (1996) Lucky Jim. In *The Strange Case of the Spotted Mice and Other Classic Essays on Science*. Oxford: Oxford University Press.
>
> Silver, B. (1998) *The Ascent of Science*. Oxford: Oxford University Press.

In the text citation, the colon after the date is followed by a page number. In some referencing systems, you might see 'p.' instead of the colon.

Here is the same passage using another style of referencing.

> Brian Silver[1] writes: 'Working within the paradigm is not necessarily second-class science.' Silver cites the discovery of DNA as an example of successful working within the paradigm. Indeed, Medawar[2] points out that Linus Pauling very nearly got there first, before Crick and Watson. The discovery depended on several other pieces of scientific work. Judgements about scientific discovery may therefore relate more to their potential future use than to whether they changed a paradigm.

At the end of the writing, the reference list is in numerical order.

1   Silver, B. *The Ascent of Science*. Oxford: Oxford University Press, 1998.

2   Medawar, P. Lucky Jim. In *The Strange Case of the Spotted Mice and Other Classic Essays on Science*. Oxford: Oxford University Press, 1996, pp. 93–102.

Here are some things to note about quoting someone else's work:

(a) What is between the quotation marks must be the author's exact words.

(b) . . . shows that something has been omitted. This should not alter the sense of what the original author has said. For example, it might be acceptable to omit a describing clause, but not a defining one.

(c) [*sic*] shows that you believe there is an error or something unorthodox but the author has actually said this (Latin for 'it is so'). It is quite often used to draw attention to inappropriate gender-biased language or use of a non-standard spelling.

(d) [ ] shows that you are adding an aside within the quote, for example an explanation. It might also be used to insert words that provide the grammatical context.

Here is an example for each.

(a) Dreyfus (2001: 106) asserts that the Internet can indeed be valuable 'as long as we continue to affirm our bodies'.

(b) Dreyfus[1] is cautiously optimistic. 'In sum, . . . the Net can be useful to us in spite of its tendency to offer the worst of a series of asymmetric trade-offs . . .'

(c) Popper draws attention to Socrates' attitude to individualism and egalitarianism: 'the belief that there is nothing more important in our life than other individual men [*sic*] . . . appears to be due to Socrates' (Popper 1962: 190).

(d) Socrates was perhaps the key early thinker about democracy. 'The greatest contribution to this faith [the open society] was to be made by Socrates who died for it.'[2]

1 Dreyfus, H. *On the Internet*. Abingdon: Routledge, 2001, p. 106.
2 Popper, K. *The Open Society and its Enemies*, 5th edn, Vol. 1. London: Routledge & Kegan Paul, 1962, p. 189.

If a quotation is long and you want to omit something, it probably helps the grammar if you look for something that is not necessary for the sense of the sentence. But you might want to think about whether you are misrepresenting the author. In example (b), I have omitted the words 'as long as we continue to affirm our bodies'. This is the crux of Dreyfus's argument and it could be misleading to leave it out.

The most important point is that if you are using someone else's exact words, then they should be put between quotation marks. This affects punctuation; if they have completed a sentence then the full stop comes within the quotation marks, as in example (d).

13.5 Double or single quotes

It really does not matter whether you use double or single quotes, unless you are following a particular style. The main thing is that you must be consistent throughout your writing. In this book, single quotes are used as standard because that is the house style of the Open University Press. If I need to quote within a quote, then I use double quotes:

> Barbara's friend Anne has tweeted, 'Notice on board is headed, "Must report to department office." Abel's name is on the list.'

If you think that you have inappropriately mixed double and single quotes – and it is easily done – you can do a search for double quotes and replace them with single ones. It is easier that way round for most word processors; the other way round might cause you to replace apostrophes, which would be a problem.

13.6 Different systems for referencing

The examples so far show the two main approaches to referencing – author-date and citation number. There are many variations on these two forms: in fact, there are thousands of referencing styles. It is no wonder that students and academic staff find it confusing. I have used the same simple example to show the different ways that something might be cited.

Gill has made a plea for a single standard referencing system.

Style	In-text
APA (American Psychological Association)	Gill (2009) has made a plea for a single standard referencing system.
Chicago	Alec Gill has made a plea for a single standard referencing system in a *Times Higher Education* article on June 25, 2009.
Harvard	Gill (2009) has made a plea for a single standard referencing system.
MLA (Modern Language Association)	Gill (2009) has made a plea for a single standard referencing system.

| Vancouver | Gill[1] has made a plea for a single standard referencing system.
OR
Gill (1) has made a plea for a single standard referencing system. |

Style	Reference list or bibliography
APA	Gill, A. (2009, June 25) There are 3,000 ways to cite source material – why not make it one? *Times Higher Education*, pp. 24–25
Chicago	Gill, A. 2009. There are 3,000 ways to cite source material – why not make it one? *Times Higher Education*, Opinion section. [Or might not be included in reference list at all.]
Harvard	Gill, A. (2009) There are 3,000 ways to cite source material – why not make it one? *Times Higher Education*, 25 June, pp. 24–25
MLA	Gill, Alec. 'There are 3,000 ways to cite source material – why not make it one?' Times Higher Education, 25 June 2009: 24+
Vancouver	Gill, A. There are 3,000 ways to cite source material – why not make it one? Times Higher Education. 2009 Jun 25; 24+

You might find alternative versions even of these styles. Notice the slight differences in punctuation, position of dates etc.

If your department has its own 'house style' then follow that to the letter, no matter what you might see elsewhere. Otherwise, there is a great deal of useful information on the Web. Try searching for: "citation style" and the name.

You should note that I've just used double quotation marks in the last paragraph, despite our house style. This is because the double quotation marks around an expression indicate that you want the search to be of the whole expression. This is one way of finding out whether an expression has been used by someone else. It is a quick way for academics to see whether someone has been plagiarizing or not.

13.7 Oh what a giveaway

Kim has returned from checking the departmental requirements about references; her department has a set of guidelines. She wonders how she managed to get to her final year without realizing this! She notices Abel's suitcase in her hall and groans inwardly. Bad news travels quickly and she has also heard the rumour that Abel and his flatmate are in some kind of trouble. She doesn't need hassle like that just now.

Kim: Hi, guys. Can't stop. I just want to format these references. Did you know there's software that does this for you? The uni's got a site licence; we don't have to pay for it if we use it on campus.

Barbara: Yeah – is it EndNote or Reference Manager? Something like that. There are some free ones too. I was just thinking it would be good for Abel, who's having to shift between different styles. You just have to key in your reference once and then tell it to output it in APA or Vancouver or whatever.

Kim: You don't even have to key it all in. You can export it from Web of Science or other databases.

Abel: Too much jargon. Stop it! Kim, Barbara's in the middle of telling me something.

Kim: Are you in some kind of trouble, Abel?

Abel: I don't think so. I haven't done anything. Don't know what Gus has been up to though – he's acting oddly.

Barbara: You've got to go to the department office tomorrow. What's that for? My friend says that it's often to do with plagiarism.

Abel: I haven't plagiarized.

Kim: Are you sure? It can happen by accident. And when you were substituting words from the thesaurus, that would have been plagiarism.

Abel: But I changed all that. I took what Brian Silver said and put it in my own words and then made a comment on it. And I acknowledged his ideas.

Barbara: Your essay's here, right? Let's google a bit just to make sure you haven't left it in by accident.

Abel opens a copy of his essay on his computer. Barbara highlights a sentence, copies it, opens up Google and pastes in the sentence. She puts double quotation marks around the sentence. She then does a search.

Barbara: Abel, this whole sentence already exists on the Internet. It's quite long. You must have copied it from somewhere.

Kim: So you have plagiarized.

13.8 In your own words

As a lecturer, I am conscious that many students plagiarize by accident. They copy what looks like useful information and then later find it in their notes and think that they have written it. I am still a student myself and I am aware of the difficulty in finding words, especially when I am on the point of understanding something. It can sometimes feel that what I am reading is the only way to say something. But I know from experience that this is the stage where I am integrating new knowledge into my repertoire – and so I need to find my own way of stating what is going on.

If you are at a UK university, then it is essential that you can find words to say something, or to comment on something that other writers have said. Students sometimes say to me, 'If we're all using the same textbook and doing the same experiments, we're bound to write exactly the same thing.' Actually, it would be very surprising if you did. For evidence that people do not write exactly the same way, you only need to look at the different referencing styles in Section 13.6. As a reader, I expect to see at least minor differences in punctuation and language use for writing that's on the same topic. If I don't, then I get suspicious.

Academic staff do not like being suspicious of their students. Some tell me that they are worried about the increased prevalence of software that 'detects' plagiarism as it gives a message that they don't trust their students. Students can also be very concerned by this software and about the idea that they might be in very severe trouble for plagiarizing unintentionally. One student thought that she might be in trouble with the police (she would not).

Having said that, increased levels of plagiarism really annoy those students who don't do it. Why should they struggle to put something together, only to get a lower mark than someone whose only skill is in copying and pasting?

So, how do you find your own words? It goes back to a point Kim made in Chapter 2: 'What exactly are you trying to say?' It can feel to some students that they are not trying to say anything; they are bringing together what other writers are saying. But even in bringing these writers together, you are making a point yourself. You are showing how what they have said contributes to your answer to the question or to your meeting your terms of reference.

If you are very tempted to plagiarize, or even to use too many direct quotations, stop looking at the other person's writing and answer the following questions:

- What is the main point?
- Why is this relevant to my topic?
- Has anyone else talked about this and agreed or disagreed with it?
- What are the implications of what this writer says?

The 'so what' question – what are the implications – is very important, especially if you are being asked to be analytical or critical. You are making a judgement about something, not just accepting it at face value.

Once you've been through this process, try writing about what the author has said, but using your own words. If you are just indicating the main point, then you are summarizing it; if you want to provide some detail, then you are paraphrasing it. Paraphrasing is legitimate, as long as you still acknowledge where the idea came from and build it into your own essay writing.

I am now going to appear to contradict myself and suggest some 'reusable language' that you can use to provide a framework for your own words. These useful expressions are empty of content, and you would be unlikely to get into trouble for using them. Even so, you should not use them without thinking – and they might prompt some further ideas. If you read articles in your own subject area carefully, you will discover some more of this type of thing.

It could be useful to think about subjects and verbs (and relevant objects):

> The essay explores . . .

Instead of essay, you might say: report, dissertation, experiment, investigation, paper, research, study, work . . .

Instead of explores, you might say: analyses, compares, examines, evaluates, exposes, focuses on, highlights, reviews . . .

> Silver writes:

Silver could be replaced by any number of authors' names or by: the author, an author, a researcher, a writer . . .

There are also many substitute verbs, depending on what you think Silver is doing: claims, explains, explores, hypothesizes . . .

If you want to talk about Silver in the past tense, because you are referring to work that is over, you could say: demonstrated, discovered, found, reported . . .

When students start writing, they often stick to the same formula and a lot of quotations are introduced in the same way, e.g. 'Silver suggests . . .'. But there are many alternatives to this. Again, ask yourself the question: what exactly is Silver trying to do? And you don't always have to begin with the subject-verb structure (though you will still need them):

> In a comparison of two scientific views, Silver highlights . . .

> By adopting the metaphor of a raft, Silver exposes . . .

The range of possibilities is extensive; I would add more but someone else (Morley 2005) has done this so well that I usually direct students to the website he maintains. This gives me an opportunity to comment on the citation of an online source. Here is that citation in two different styles.

APA
Morley, J (2005). Academic Phrasebank. Retrieved June 27, 2009, from University of Manchester website: www.phrasebank.manchester.ac.uk

Vancouver
Morley, J, Academic Phrasebank. The University of Manchester; 2005 April 20 [cited 2009 June 27]. Available from:
www.phrasebank.manchester.ac.uk

Some styles will ask you to include the date of the last update; it is also good practice to show the date when you accessed it, as it is likely to have changed since then.

I strongly recommend that you have a look at the Academic Phrasebank if you are struggling for ways to express things in your own words. It will give you some prompts without encouraging you to plagiarize. It is also very good for your understanding of grammar to think about how phrases work.

13.9 Comments on questions

13.9.1 Why do we use references in academic writing?

The main reason is to avoid academic dishonesty. By academic dishonesty, I mean passing someone else's writing off as your own. When people read something with their own work in it, unattributed, they understandably feel upset. Universities know that they will have a bad reputation if they permit it to happen. Another important reason is to provide sufficient information for the reader to find out more about the interesting work you have cited.

13.9.2 Can you name any major citation styles?

There are many of these. Some of the commonly used ones are: APA, Chicago, Harvard, MLA, Vancouver.

13.9.3 What are the main differences between bibliographic citation and footnoting?

Bibliographic citation refers to a list of references or *bibliography* at the end. A footnote will give information about the book at the bottom of the page. Sometimes this information is in a list of notes at the end of the book. With bibliographic citation, the list may be in alphabetical order. If numbers have been used in the text, the list will be in numerical order.

A bibliography, such as the one at the end of this book, is not necessarily composed of references: it could refer to books not directly referenced in the text. The terms 'References' and 'Bibliography' are, however, used interchangeably by academics in higher education, adding to the confusion! You should assume that it is a list of references (works cited) that staff want unless they tell you otherwise.

If your list of references is in alphabetical order, then that should apply to the whole list, include websites and journal articles.

13.9.4 What is the difference between direct and indirect citation?

Direct citation involves quotation marks and the exact words of the author. Indirect citation, which is used more frequently by academic writers, acknowledges the original author's ideas but paraphrases or summarizes them in the current author's own words.

13.9.5 Is it plagiarism if you paraphrase or translate someone else's work?

It may not be, if you acknowledge that you are doing this and do not attempt to pass it off as your own. This would apply only to small sections of material, properly acknowledged and integrated into your argument. A complete translation or paraphrase of someone else's paper would not be acceptable. It is not an academic essay or other piece of original writing.

13.9.6 How would you make reference to this book?

How you answer this question will depend on the referencing style you are using. The information you need to answer the question can be found in the inside cover. Here are two versions of answers:

APA style
Students should not be sneered at for their lack of knowledge about grammar (Sinclair, 2010).

Sinclair, C. (2010). *Grammar: a friendly approach* (2nd ed.). Maidenhead: Open University Press.

Vancouver style
Knowing about grammar may help students with their referencing.[1]

1   Sinclair C. Grammar: a friendly approach. 2nd ed. Maidenhead: Open University Press, 2010.

13.10 Conclusion: advice about avoiding plagiarism

- If you copy anything from any source at any time, make sure you know where it comes from.
- If you think you (or someone else) might have copied something, try googling a phrase from it in double quotation marks. It is not guaranteed to find everything, but is a useful starting point.
- Learn how to *summarize* and paraphrase.
- Keep asking yourself, 'What is it I am trying to say?'
- Make sure you understand the referencing conventions used by your department.
- Pay special attention to the punctuation required in your citation style.
- The main advice about plagiarism is DON'T DO IT!

13.10.1 Technical terms relating to this chapter

For further information, look up these words or phrases in the Glossary, other grammar books or the World Wide Web.

> Bibliography
> *Bibliographic software*
> Citation styles
> Paraphrase
> Plagiarism
> *Plagiarism software*
> Reference
> Referencing conventions
> *Sic*
> Summarize

There are many useful resources on the Internet that will help you to avoid plagiarism, some of which are updated regularly.

14

The machine's out to get us

14.1 Technology makes it possible • 14.2 Questions about technology in grammar and language • 14.3 Catching plagiarism – or helping to avoid it • 14.4 Should computers mark essays? • 14.5 Friendly computing: assistive technology • 14.6 The human touch • 14.7 Comments on questions • 14.8 Conclusion: comments on technology and grammar

14.1 Technology makes it possible

Kim's off doing her presentation. Barbara wanted to go with her to give her moral support, but Abel seems to need her even more. They are looking at an official letter, telling Abel that he has been caught plagiarizing and colluding.

Abel:	Listen, Barbara, I swear to you – again – that I didn't plagiarize. I nearly did it by mistake. What's colluding, anyway? I'm being accused of something I don't understand.
Barbara:	It's about conspiring – it involves someone else. Gus in this case, I think.
Abel:	I've never conspired with Gus. I realized quickly that I don't really like him. He takes my stuff and disses my friends. I hardly talk to him except to ask for things back.
Barbara:	Did you work together on the essay on paradigms? Remember I found a sentence on the Internet.

Abel: No. I got a much better grade than him for a start. So that can't be it.

Barbara: But the Turnitin analysis apparently shows several sentences appear in both your essays. Did you give him your essay? Maybe in an earlier draft – one that had the dodgy bits in.

Abel: No, I wouldn't do that, Barbara. And anyway, how would it get on the Internet?

Barbara: We never looked at that properly; perhaps we should.

She searches with the offending sentence again and then goes to the site where it is repeated. It's in a file that looks like an essay, but there is no name on it.

Abel: That's it! That'll be Gus's essay. He puts them all on his website; goodness knows why. He must want the world to know how stupid he is.

He takes over from Barbara and finds Gus's website.

Abel: Yes, here's the link to his essays. And here's the one with that sentence in it. Wow, it does have a lot of my stuff in it; he's even got 'tergiversation'. What a giveaway!

Barbara: What happened when your laptop got a virus?

Abel: Oh, he had it for ages. I'd backed everything up so I did the rest of the essay on other people's computers. So he must have found my essay and just nicked it.

Barbara: So does that let you off the hook?

Abel: I'd hope so. But I'm not sure about this collusion stuff. Perhaps I'm still responsible.

Eddie arrives at the door. His dissertation is handed in and he's nearly in party mode.

Barbara: Oh, it's you. You're doing law; perhaps you can help us with our problem. If Abel's flatmate steals his essay, is it OK for Abel to murder him?

14.2 Questions about technology in grammar and language

1 How are advances in technology changing the way we speak and write?
2 What is the main function of plagiarism software (such as *Turnitin*)?

3 Would you prefer a computer or a human being to mark your essay?
4 What is *assistive technology*?

There are comments on these question in Section 14.7.

14.3 Catching plagiarism – or helping to avoid it

There are several software packages on the market now that will check the originality of an essay. Turnitin, one of the best known ones, takes pains to stress that it isn't about detection but about prevention. This software is now being used in universities across the UK, in some very different ways, by both staff and students.

The package works by showing whether a new piece of writing contains material that is similar to or exactly the same as other pieces of writing. It allows people to look at writing side-by-side to compare whether this work has appeared in anything else that is available elsewhere. The new piece of writing then joins the database of existing writing and can in turn be compared against future pieces.

Thus when Gus stole Abel's draft essay and put it on his website, he exposed it in two ways: when the essays were marked and put through Turnitin, they would show up as having similarities. But they might also show up because a version was already on the Internet. In addition, any quotations used will trigger the comparison; this is known about and built into the way people interpret the findings of the software.

There are some debates about this software in the academic community. Some feel that it is very useful as a deterrent; others feel it encourages students to work out how to get round the software! It is sometimes used as a teaching tool to help students to 'see' when plagiarism arises by accident.

The main purpose in mentioning it here is to point out that it is quite likely being used on your writing if you are attending a UK university. If you have not plagiarized, then you should have nothing to fear. It should always be possible to demonstrate that something is your own work; for a start, you will be able to talk about how you produced your writing. If you think that you may have plagiarized by accident, then this should encourage you to go over your work carefully to remove anything that might be seen in this light.

I haven't yet used the software myself. I have grown from being a very naive new lecturer who didn't realize that people did this, to a very savvy older lecturer who can spot it a mile away! I can also usually tell the difference between accidental plagiarism and deliberate stealing and cheating. This book gives away a couple of my secrets, but I have many more. But I am now thinking about using the software, as much to help students to avoid plagiarism as to detect and punish it.

14.4 Should computers mark essays?

Even though I don't use the Turnitin software myself, I can see how it speeds up some processes. If I suspect plagiarism, I have to take the trouble to find out and this may possibly involve interviewing the student. One of the advantages of automation is that it can make comparisons very quickly, thus removing some of the drudgery.

There are other automated processes with such benefits. Computers are getting better and better at checking spelling and grammar (despite my warnings in Chapter 12). They provide very easy ways to search for specific terms that you might expect to see in a student's essay. They provide useful databases, for storing references or banks of comments on students' essays. Why not just hand over to them completely and let them mark the essays?

I am happy to use computers to help with some of these tasks, but personally would have problems in handing them over completely. As we saw with the grammar checker, if you don't know whether the checker is right with its suggestion, it is risky to accept it. While students do often express a wish for more consistency in marking – which would happen with *automated essay grading* – many feel that they would rather write for a person than for a machine.

In the course I am taking myself as a student, which is entirely online, my tutors send me feedback using *text annotations* to my essay. I find this very helpful: I can see at a glance what they are commenting on; I don't have to read their handwriting; I don't feel that they have vandalized my script. It feels like the dialogue that I like to see between different people engaged at different levels on the same topic.

So I am not against the use of technology to help with grammar, spelling, language use, feedback, checking standards and honesty. Plagiarism prevention software, such as Turnitin, is now developing to incorporate opportunities for peer feedback, and customized feedback, and all this should support improvements in use of language and grammar. As long as the human beings aren't left out altogether, these developments are very positive.

14.5 Friendly computing: assistive technology

Automation brings problems and advantages for people with a disability. If new technology is not properly designed, it can exclude people – perhaps they are unable to see, hear, reach or move the particular pieces of equipment. On the positive side, new technology has brought more creative solutions to old ways of doing things, allowing people to see what others hear, for example.

Tools developed to support disability are now proving very helpful for all users. Examples in our current context might include mind-mapping, word-prediction and text-to-speech software, all of which can help with the presentation, planning and structuring of ideas and language.

Students with a disability might want to mention the TechDis website to staff at their university. The site helpfully displays how it should be cited, i.e.

> Staff supporting Students. Techdis URL: http://www.techdis.ac.uk/index/php?p=6_3 Viewed 28 Jun 2009

14.6 The human touch

Poor Abel. He has been working really hard, but he has been ill, skint, nearly homeless, unlucky in love – and now he's accused of plagiarism. It doesn't seem as though Eddie will cheer him up much.

Eddie: Mm, collusion is quite serious. I knew a couple who were chucked out for it. They handed in the same essay. They both got the blame, even though she was the one that had done most of the copying. He got chucked out too. Women!

Barbara: Typical! How do you know she'd done most of the copying? Anyway, Gus isn't a woman – and he stole it! He didn't just copy it.

Eddie: Is he going to 'fess up?

Abel: I don't know. I've fallen out with him. I knew nothing about it. I've only just found out.

Eddie: Have you kept all your drafts?

Abel: Yes, it's all here on this flashdrive. And on Barbara's computer. And Kim's too, although it did some weird things to my files.

Eddie: The weird things to the files might help you prove your case. Get it all backed up. And make sure that you don't obliterate any dates for things. I think you've got a strong case. Mind you, you wouldn't have if you had known that he had taken it.

Barbara: Really? If he copies it from me, then I get chucked out too? No way. We're always borrowing each others' laptops.

Eddie: 'Fraid so. So don't go lending any of your assignments to anyone.

Barbara: Right, let's make sure that these computers come up with all the evidence we need. I think that we can use our knowledge of grammar and punctuation to prove that Abel got there first. I'm not going to let a computer program chuck my grammar pal out of university!

14.7 Comments on questions

14.7.1 How are advances in technology changing the way we speak and write?

These changes have been happening ever since human beings first learned to write and changed the way they used memory and stories. Currently, the changes seem to be that people have access to a great deal more information – and this is changing how they process it. As an example, referencing software gives us immediate access to many different styles of referencing, but the proliferation of these styles is making life very confusing, especially for students. The use of the mobile phone is encouraging more writing, but it is writing that has many features of spoken language. This may result in some changes to our communications of which we are not yet aware. Some problems of communications across the generations – e.g. between university academics and their students – have been noticed because of use of text language.

14.7.2 What is the main function of plagiarism software (such as Turnitin)?

The main function claimed is the prevention of plagiarism. However, universities undoubtedly use it for detection as well.

14.7.3 Would you prefer a computer or a human being to mark your essay?

Obviously, this is a personal question. Some people think that a computer would be more reliable and therefore more fair. Many think that this would depersonalize the relationship between staff and students. My own view is that it might provide some useful information to help me with my marking, but I would never hand over all the responsibility to a computer.

14.7.4 What is assistive technology?

This is the name given to technology that creates enabling environments to allow everyone to participate fully in daily activities. There is a wide range of assistive technology for students with a disability at university. This includes not only spellcheckers and grammar checkers, but also word prediction, screen-readers, mind-mapping software. There is also assistive technology built into many standard packages, applications and systems. Have a look at your system preferences and see if you can find what's available on your own computer.

14.8 Conclusion: comments on technology and grammar

- Technology can be used not only for automation of tasks, but also for liberating us to enable us to extend our skills and knowledge through greater access to information.
- With respect to grammar, technology is valuable for checking your work or for assessing the originality of someone else's work – but only if you understand what it is telling you.
- The main purpose of this chapter is to alert you to current and future uses of technology with respect to grammar and language use.

14.8.1 Technical terms relating to this chapter

For further information, look up these words in the Glossary or the World Wide Web. They are unlikely to be in other grammar books, but they seem very relevant to the friendly approach to grammar.

Assistive technology
Automated essay grading
Text annotation
Turnitin

15

Finale

Our students are getting ready for Kim's party. For Abel, this means changing his T-shirt. He's not into dressing up, especially in kinky stuff associated with the *Rocky Horror Picture Show*, and he can't afford to anyway. He's relieved that Eddie was right; his case for not being guilty of collusion or plagiarism was fairly easy to prove and was dropped immediately when he presented the evidence. He is thinking that he has learned quite a lot about human nature as well as grammar this semester.

As Kim dresses up as Frank N. Furter, she reflects on the difference between today and yesterday. Yesterday, she was in a smart suit impressing industrial sponsors with her talk about the role of engineering in environmental improvement. It was very successful; there were no wrong past participles and her passion for the subject shone through in her well-prepared talk. She will probably get sponsorship to do a PhD. Today, she will be the centre of attention again – in the role of a mad scientist from the planet Transsexual. She looks at the apostrophe on a stick and decides to take it with her to the film and the party. It will go with the whip. She has promised the police and her friends not to be quite so expressive in correcting people in future, and these are just props.

Barbara has a lot to think about: outrageous costume, make-up, props for the film (she's taking toast, rice and a newspaper), the bag with Kim's birthday presents. And, most importantly, she has her list of put-downs for grammar snobs. She spent half the night with Derek making this up. Here they are:

- It is surely pedantic to puritanically avoid the *split infinitive*.
- If I were you, I'd forget about the *subjunctive*.
- Between you and me, I'm not sure that we need to use the *accusative case* after *prepositions* . . .
- . . . but if you want *hypercorrection*, then we'll say it's between you and I.
- I hope my using a *gerund* doesn't confuse you.

- I shall insist on the correct use of *'shall' or 'will'*. You will help me.
- I won't think less of you if you give me fewer adverbs.
- I think a preposition is the best thing to end a sentence with.
- To whom am I speaking anyway?
- Kingsley Amis might describe me as a berk, but we know what he'd say about you!

If you want to know more about Barbara's put-downs, check them in the Glossary, the Internet and other grammar books. The main point about them is that they contain examples of what they are talking about: she's showing she knows the 'correct' version but is trying to suggest that the snob is being unnecessarily fussy.

What Kingsley Amis (see Bibliography) said is the opposite of 'berk' is too rude for this book, so you'll have to look it up somewhere else.

Barbara's put-downs are a bit too sneery as a message for this book, though in the final scene you can see that preparing them has helped her score a few points over Calum at the party. Abel's been making a list that might be more useful: this is called Warning Signs, and it can be seen in Figure 15.1.

After the film, a large number of weirdly dressed students cram into Kim's flat. As Kim plays the saxophone, Barbara finds herself in a line doing the 'time warp' between Calum and Mark.

Calum: Ah, the grammar girl. The one who won't stand in the queue in Marks and Spencer that says 'five items or less'.

Barbara: Just give me fewer comparative adverbs.

Calum: I heard you were pretty hot on the subjunctive too.

Barbara: Isn't that what Kim's playing just now? If I were you, I'd keep quiet about it.

Calum: Very good. And where do you stand on the gerund?

Barbara: I wouldn't want to hurt it. My standing on it would probably kill it.

Mark: It's supposed to be a party – what's that guy talking about?

Barbara: Oh well, Kingsley Amis had a word for him. *[She turns to talk to Mark.]* Thanks for rescuing Kim, by the way. And for the tweets.

Mark: Sorry I wasn't in touch before. My dad had a heart attack in November and I've been looking after the shop. Not easy when you've a load of essays to do. But he's a lot better now, as you saw.

Barbara: Sorry to hear that. I wondered what had happened.

Mark: I told him I'd be going out with less girls next semester – just the one, if she'll have me.

Barbara: Fewer girls. Oh sorry – I didn't mean to . . .

Mark:	OK, let's start again. And this time, no cheating, no standing up – and no sneering.
Barbara:	I'm fine with that.

Kim puts down her saxophone and goes over to Abel. He's sitting in a corner looking glum.

Kim:	Abel – what are you playing at? Barbara's over there; why aren't you getting together? I might as well let you know, I'm trying to write a romantic story about you – to enter a competition. I need a little crisis, yes, to make the story interesting – but a queasy stomach, plagiarism and being skint is just not going to do it. I want a proper story.
Abel:	Well, hasn't she gone off with that rich guy, Calum, anyway? And what story? Haven't you got enough to do?
Kim:	I just wanted to try a different kind of writing. A romantic fiction – I had a story about two people falling in love over a participle.
Abel:	Oh really!
Kim:	It was like a break from engineering – writing I enjoyed doing. And I liked that. Especially when I realized what fun punctuation could be. Thanks for the 'phonetic punctuation' by the way. That was your idea, wasn't it? It didn't seem like a Barbara thing. It's dead funny, but he's kind of right in a way – you can almost hear commas and things sometimes.
Abel:	Yeah, I like Victor Borge. But I thought you'd like it because of the way you saw punctuation kind of like music. I'm really getting interested in different ways of teaching people things.

An attractive stranger walks past and hears this.

Sari:	You can teach me English. I ask Eddie but he don't tell me things. I'm Sari. Eddie invited me – hope it OK. He say I need practise English.
Abel:	Your English sounds very good.
Sari:	Can't do articles – 'the' and 'a'. Not have in my language. And single and plural not good.
Kim:	There we are. You can teach English and grammar, Abel. I'll have to find something else to write about – I'm too late for the competition anyway. And Barbara . . . *[Barbara comes up beside her as she says this]*
Barbara:	. . . Barbara what?
Kim:	You'll make your mark somehow.
Abel:	Tell you what, Sari – I'm drawing up a list of 'Warning Signs'; things I know I make mistakes with. Can I run it past you? I'm free tomorrow.
Barbara:	Listen. Mark's had a great idea. We've all been writing some of this

> grammar stuff down and people are getting interested in it. Why don't we write a book and sell it?
>
> Kim: Like, *Grammar Without Sneering*?
>
> Barbara: Something like that, yeah.
>
> Abel: No, the title's got to have a colon in it. I like colons now.
>
> Barbara: How about *Grammar: A Friendly Approach*?
>
> Kim: It'll never work.

What I might write	What might be wrong	Comment
there	Perhaps it should be 'their' or 'they're'	Best to make it 'they are', rather than 'they're'
,	It might not be strong enough or it might not be necessary.	I make this kind of decision at proofreading stage
definitely	I might spell it with an a instead of the second i	It has 'finite' in the middle
separate	I might spell it with an e instead of the first a	It has 'a rat' in the middle
desperate	I might spell it with an a instead of the second e	I remember the Latin for 'I hope' is 'spero' – this helps me to spell it.
it's	It should be 'its'	Never write 'it's' – replace it with 'it is'
where	It should be 'were'	Actually, I don't do this. Because I have a Scottish accent, I 'hear' a difference between these two words. But so many students, including Scottish ones, do this that I thought I'd put it in the list.
a very long sentence	There are many unnecessary words.	I do this one a lot. I then go back over it to see if I can shorten it.

Figure 15.1   Warning signs

16

Glossary

Don't feel intimidated by this list of words; you don't need to know them all. The definitions are given in case you need an explanation for a word you encounter, for example it might have been used in feedback from a lecturer. In the examples, I have sometimes provided an illustration of a grammatical point and have put this in italics.

Word	Definition and notes	Examples
abbreviation	Shortened word or expression. The example shows the abbreviation 'i.e.' used correctly (see Chapter 10). See also *acronym*, *apostrophe* and *full stop*.	The students had matriculated at the university, *i.e.* they had enrolled with Registry.
academic English	The kind of English used in learned journals and conference papers, and expected of university students in their essays, reports etc. It is often referred to in the context of second language users, but is relevant to all participants in university life. There are different variants of this style of English in different subject areas. See Chapter 3.	A *critical review* of a journal article suggested it would be very appropriate for the scientific community. (Critical in this sense does not necessarily mean negative or hostile.)
accusative case	The form of a noun or pronoun that shows that it is an object. While this is common in many languages, it is rare in English but still exists in words such as 'me', which is the accusative case of 'I'.	She helped *me*. In fact, she helped *Barbara and me*.
acronym	An abbreviation made up of initial letters or parts of words that has now become a word in its own right.	What would we do without *radar*? Most people know that *AIDS* is an acronym; did you know that *amphetamine* is too?

Word	Definition and notes	Examples
active voice	The form of verb where the subject undertakes the action of the sentence. Compare *passive voice* and see also Chapter 8.	Abel *questions* his ability to become a teacher.
adjective	A word that describes a noun, pronoun or other adjective.	Kim has very *happy* memories of her party.
adverb	A word that explains how a verb was undertaken (modifies a verb).	Barbara went *happily* to her resit exam.
adverbial clause	A subordinate clause that explains the action of the main clause. See Chapter 6 for useful conjunctions for introducing adverbial clauses.	He helped me *when I forgot my book.*
agreement	The condition that subjects and verbs match each other in terms of singular and plural. See Chapter 2.	*Abel goes* to the gym; *Kim and Barbara go* to the pub.
apostrophe '	Punctuation mark indicating possession or missing letters. See Chapter 11.	I'll meet *Barbara's* friend at 6 o'clock.
Apostrophe Protection Society	A society dedicated to the proper use of the apostrophe.	The Apostrophe Protection Society's website can be found at www.apostrophe.org.uk
article	An adjective showing whether a noun is indefinite or definite.	Kim is *an* engineering student. Barbara is *the* student who studies English.
assistive technology	Technology that gives assistance to people with a disability; it may also have wider application. See Chapter 14.	'Assistive technology can be anything that can be used to support your specific needs – from the spellchecker in Word to a Braille Embosser.' (Disability Service, University of Strathclyde)
automated essay grading	Use of technology that checks essays and provides feedback, based on how typical academics in the subject would mark the essay; the software 'learns' from the tutors. This is discussed briefly in Chapter 14.	We all know that multiple choice questions are easily marked by a computer; now there are many commercial systems that try to do the same thing with free responses. One example is PEG (Project Essay Grade).
auxiliary verb	Verb that is used with a participle to help show the tense and mood of the action. See Chapter 5.	I *should have* finished writing my dissertation by the time I go to the party.
bibliographic software	Software that allows you to store your references in a database, import new ones from the Internet, and output these references in any style you want. This is invaluable for referencing. See Chapter 13.	Students who use Web of Knowledge in their Athens accounts can export what they find there to their own bibliographic software.

bibliography	A list of books and other reference materials; these may have been consulted during the course of a piece of writing. Compare *references*.	The tutor handed out a list of key books on the subject with comments on their usefulness – an annotated bibliography.
bracket [ ]	A punctuation mark, used in pairs, to show that something is enclosed and separated off. See Figure 10.3.	Barbara said, 'He *[Abel]* will be along when he's finished playing tennis.'
citation styles	Styles of referencing that follow specific conventions; even within these, however, there may be slight differences in practice. Examples of these styles can be see in Chapter 13.	On the WorldCat website, you can choose to export or copy what you have found in one of several different styles.
cite	Quote or make reference to. See especially Chapter 13.	When you cite an author, the reader should be able to find the original source.
clause	A group of words containing a verb (compare *phrase*).	Abel wants to be a teacher *because he enjoys a challenge*.
colon :	A punctuation mark that introduces something, such as a list, a quote or an explanation. See Figure 10.3.	Barbara has made a big decision: she is going to major in philosophy.
comma ,	A punctuation mark that separates or encloses. See especially Chapter 10 and Figure 10.3.	Abel said, '*Barbara*, I'd like some help with *commas, semicolons* and full stops.'
comma splice	The error of using a comma to separate two main clauses. See especially Chapter 7; this is also mentioned as one of lecturers' pet hates in Chapter 1.	There is a comma splice in the following sentence: 'Kim has invited Mark to her *party, this* is because he rescued her.' It would be better to put a semicolon or full stop after 'party'.
complement	A completion for certain types of verb that can't take an object, e.g. to be. See Chapters 4 and 6.	Kim is *a third year student*.
complex sentence	A sentence that has at least one subordinate clause. See Chapter 6.	Barbara is upset *when she sees that Kim has already got the book*.
compound sentence	A sentence that has at least two main clauses. See Chapter 6.	*Barbara is upset* and *she shouts at Abel*.
compound subject	The subject of the sentence that has two or more agents. This has implications for agreement. See Chapter 4.	*Philosophy*, which is Barbara's subject, *and the philosophy of science* represent two of the discourses considered in this book.
conjunction	A word that joins two main clauses or a subordinate clause to a main sentence. See Chapter 6.	Kim likes music *but* Abel prefers sport. Barbara likes neither, *though* she goes for the company.
co-ordinating conjunction	A word that joins two main clauses, such as 'and' or 'but'. See Figure 6.1.	The essay is late *but* the lecturer has a lot of marking *and* he won't notice.

Word	Definition and notes	Examples
count noun	A noun that refers to something that can be counted. It can use words like 'a' and 'fewer'.	We can talk about a *song* and fewer *songs*, but we have to say some music and less music.
dangling participle	A participle that is not related to its auxiliary verb or subject. See Section 5.3. This is more formally known as a misrelated participle.	*Drinking* in the last chance saloon. This doesn't make sense unless someone is doing the drinking, e.g. Abel is drinking in the last chance saloon.
dash –	A punctuation mark that is used to introduce a change or significant point, or, in pairs, to enclose. See Figure 10.3.	Barbara – *our youngest student* – learned more grammar at school than the others.
	There are various lengths of dash and longer ones are used to show that something is missing, for example if you don't want to give someone's full name.	*Kim W*—— was arrested today.
definite article	The definite article is 'the'. See *article*.	*The* dream that Martin Luther King had was about true equality and freedom.
dependent clause	Another word for subordinate clause. You know the clause is dependent because of the presence of a conjunction or relative pronoun. See Chapters 6, 7 and 9.	I will be coming out *unless it is raining*.
dialect	Use of language and grammar that belongs to a particular region of the country or group of people. (This is not the same as accent – it is more to do with the words used.) See Chapter 2.	In some dialects, the singular and plural forms are reversed from the Standard English version. Thus we might hear: '*We was* robbed; *it were* a travesty.'
ellipsis . . .	A punctuation mark indicating missing words or a fading away.	Such an expression 'will forever *be* . . . *one* of Santa's little helpers' (Truss 2003).
finite verb	A complete verb that has a subject and a tense and also indicates person (first, second or third person). See especially Chapter 5.	Barbara *will be going* to the party when she *has found* a suitable costume.
fragment	An incomplete sentence, containing no finite verb, or having an unlinked joining word. See especially Chapter 7. A grammar checker will sometimes pick this up (see Chapter 12).	*Being a fan of Gothic outfits. Though she hasn't found a good costume yet.* Neither of these would be sentences, even if they made sense in the context of the previous sentence.

freewriting	A technique to help writers to overcome blocks; write for a set time, in sentences, without stopping. See Elbow (1973) and Murray (2006) in the Bibliography.	I try to write for five minutes in my journal each morning so that I can find out what I'm thinking about. No one ever sees my freewriting.
full stop .	A punctuation mark used to show the end of a sentence or an abbreviation (see Chapter 10). It is also known as a period.	This sentence should end in a *full stop*. We use good grammar, *e.g.* appropriate participles.
genitive case	The version of a noun or pronoun that shows it is possessive. This is common in some languages, but in English it has resulted in the apostrophe (and caused some confusion in the process). 'Girles' would originally have been the genitive of 'girls' – thus 'girles books'. Now, however, an apostrophe is inserted to show the missing letter (e). (See *possessive*.)	The genitive case can be seen in the following expressions: It's *Barbara's* chocolate. It's *her* chocolate. The chocolate is *hers*. The problem is *yours*. The second example shows a *possessive adjective*.
genre	A recognizable type or style, often used in relation to films, e.g. Western, Bollywood, romcom.	In academic writing, you are expected to use the genre of the academic essay in your subject area.
gerund	A noun made from a verb, usually a present participle.	The *changing* of the guard is a popular spectacle for tourists.
greengrocer's apostrophe	An expression used to describe the prevalence of inappropriate apostrophes used with simple plurals. See Chapter 11.	Kim painted out the apostrophes in the words *pea's, potatoe's, and pomegranate's.*
hedging	Softening words used to reduce the level of certainty being expressed. While too much hedging can result in vagueness, it can be useful to introduce an element of doubt sometimes. Modal auxiliaries are particularly helpful for this (see Chapter 5).	Abel *may have taken* an interest in Sari.
hypercorrection	Wrong correction based on following a 'rule' that shouldn't apply. A typical example is when people want to avoid saying 'me' because they were told as children not to say 'Him and me want to go out.' A useful rule is that if you would say 'me' naturally if it were just you, then you should also do so when it is you and someone else, e.g. 'If it is up to Barbara and me, then we'll go for the chocolate.'	Some people say that '*between you and I*' is hypercorrection; others ask why 'between' should take the accusative case just because it does in Latin. 'Between you and me' is still regarded as the correct version, however.

Word	Definition and notes	Examples
hyphen -	Punctuation mark joining words or parts of words, especially to avoid confusion. See Chapter 10.	Kim wrote a *post-Horror* letter to Eddie.
idiom	The way things are said by a particular group of people. See Chapter 2.	I shall *table* an item at the meeting. (Literally, put on the table.) This is an idiom to say I shall want to talk about an issue but will not send out a paper in advance of the meeting. The verb 'to table' is not used in any other way. We do not table our cups and saucers.
indefinite article	Indefinite articles are 'a' or 'an'. See *article*.	'I have *a* dream' (Martin Luther King).
indefinite pronoun	Pronouns that don't stand for specific identifiable people: e.g. *any, anyone, some, something, none, each, either, many* (there is quite a long list).	You can't come on Wednesday or Thursday; *neither* is suitable. (Note that 'neither' is singular.)
infinitive	The 'to' form of the verb.	Barbara is happy *to write* in a formal style.
inflection	Variation in word ending which says something about number, person, tense etc.	The inflection in a word such as '*writes*' shows that it is the *third person singular*.
interjection	A part of speech that covers exclamations. You are unlikely to use these in academic writing generally – though they would be of specialist interest, e.g. to anthropologists or linguists.	It has been noted that students from certain universities say '*hurrah!*' while others say '*hurray!*'.
intransitive verb	A verb that doesn't take an object. See Chapter 5. Many verbs have both transitive and intransitive forms, e.g. play, run, write, smell. The possibility of a verb being either transitive or intransitive is behind the old joke: My dog's got no nose. How does he smell (transitive)? Awful! (Regarding 'smell' as intransitive.)	Barbara *hesitates*. Abel *complains*. Kim *disappears*.
inverted comma ' ' or " "	A punctuation mark always found in pairs that encloses direct speech, a quotation or words that require some other form of attention. Also known as quote or quotation mark. See Figure 10.3. Chapter 13 shows how they are used to avoid plagiarism.	Kim has a complaint about Barbara and Abel. '*They're* not behaving romantically, so how can I write my story "*Love and prepositions*"?' she asks.

	Note that it is conventional to use double inverted commas when performing an Internet search on more than one word.	
metaphor	A figure of speech in which one thing is said to be another – the substitution drawing attention to particular aspects of the situation. The example uses a metaphor from law: there is no actual jury involved. See also *simile*.	*The jury is out* over whether grammar books should describe usage or prescribe it.
misrelated participle	See *dangling participle*.	
modal auxiliaries	Verbs used to express mood – for example, showing doubt, necessity, duty. See Chapter 5.	Kim *ought to* concentrate on her dissertation instead of writing stories.
non-count noun	See *count noun*.	
non-restrictive clause	A relative clause that describes rather than defines part of the main clause. See Chapter 9. It usually follows a comma or is enclosed in a pair of commas.	Abel now owns a thesaurus, *which has contributed to his problems*.
noun	A word that names a person, thing, place, idea, emotion. Nouns can be abstract, i.e. they do not refer to an actual physical thing.	*Scientists* tend to prefer abstract *nouns* to *verbs*; thus they will talk about a *substitution* rather than say 'we substituted'.
noun clause	A subordinate clause that has the function of a noun.	Barbara described *what she was going to do*.
object	The person or thing that receives the action of a verb. There are also indirect objects, where someone or something is affected by the action, e.g. Barbara in the second example. See Chapter 6.	Kim plays *the saxophone*. Abel gives Barbara *a chocolate*.
paraphrase	Express the same thing in your own words – a useful skill to avoid plagiarism. See Chapter 13 and compare with *summarize*.	To paraphrase an expression: beauty depends on who is making the judgement (paraphrasing 'beauty is in the eye of the beholder').
parenthesis	The act of enclosing, using any of the pairs of enclosing marks shown in Figure 10.3. In the plural, it also refers to the round brackets *(parentheses)* used to enclose an aside.	The following list uses parentheses to indicate responsibility: buying Kim's bag and chocolate *(Barbara)*; tidying Kim's flat *(Derek)*; making a final check of Kim's dissertation *(Abel)*.
participle	A part of a verb. For more details see *past participle* and *present participle*. See also Chapter 5.	The participles of the verb 'to write' are '*writing*' and '*written*'.

Word	Definition and notes	Examples
passive voice	The form of a verb where the subject has something done to it. Compare *active voice* and see Chapter 8.	Abel *was questioned* about his timekeeping.
past participle	A part of the verb used to make up tenses and also the passive voice. In regular verbs, it ends in -d or -ed, but there are many irregular verbs. See Chapter 5.	We have *worked* well and have *written* a lot. We were *praised* for this yesterday and are *expected* to do more today.
PDP	PDP stands for personal development planning, a process of reflection and planning to support learning and professionalism. See Chapter 8.	In some subjects, all students are required to complete a reflective journal as part of their PDP.
perfect tense	The tense of a verb that expresses completion in the past. See Chapter 5.	Kim *has written* her speech.
period.	Another word for 'full stop'.	A sentence ends with a *period*.
person	The form of the verb and its associated subject that indicates who or what is involved. First: *I am, we are* Second: *you are* Third: *he/she/it/one is, they are/ everybody is*	Essays should be written in the third person; that is, there should be no use of the words *I, we* or *you*.
phrase	A group of words that goes together; some say it does not contain a verb, but others disagree; however, it is not the same as a clause.	The phrase '*terms of reference*' is a useful one to think about in report writing.
plagiarism	Passing off someone's work as one's own. It is mentioned initially in Chapter 2 because of the dangers of using a thesaurus to substitute some words for others; this would still be considered plagiarism. For the second edition of this book, it has taken on a bigger role and Chapter 13 is devoted to the topic.	If I said that a subordinate clause is one of *Santa's little assistants*, I would be plagiarizing Martin Jarvis and Lynne Truss. The expression 'Santa's little helper' is an example of idiom, and that would give me away.
plagiarism software	Software that aims at the prevention or avoidance of plagiarism; it may also be used in its detection. See Chapter 14.	Turnitin is used widely in UK universities to detect and prevent plagiarism.
pluperfect	The tense used to show action before another action already in the past.	Barbara *had met* Mark in Freshers Week and was annoyed when he didn't keep in touch.

possessive	Showing that one thing belongs to or relates to another. The genitive case is also known as the possessive case.	Possessives can be seen in adjectives (*my*), pronouns (*mine*) and nouns (the *students'* grammar).
possessive adjective	When a possessive pronoun is before a noun, then it is often called a possessive adjective.	It is *my* understanding that *his* decision is to go.
possessive pronoun	Pronouns that indicate possession may be used as adjectives (as above) or may stand alone. This is possibly where some confusion comes in, especially if the word ends up being similar to another. See *pronoun*.	It is *her* decision. The decision is *hers*. She's *nobody's* fool.
predicate	What is said about the subject of a sentence, including a verb.	The students *like to study grammar occasionally* but they *prefer to watch football and go to parties*.
preposition	A word showing relationship between nouns (or their equivalent), e.g. position, movement etc., circumstances. They often occur in phrases and may include more than one word, e.g. *in front of*.	International students are often confused with idiom associated with prepositions: *by* mistake *in* error *on* purpose interest *in* objection *to* enthusiasm *for*
present participle	A part of the verb used to make up continuous forms of tenses. It ends in -ing. It is often the cause of sentence fragments and students sometimes have problems spelling the word. See Chapters 5 and 7.	Kim has been *writing* a romantic story about Barbara and Abel.
pronoun	A word that stands instead of a noun. There are several different kinds: personal, indefinite, demonstrative, interrogative and relative. They may be subjects, objects or possessive.	*I* have been writing a story about students *whose* grammar needs some work. *I* have tried to make *them* realistic. *This* is because grammar should be part of life, not separated from *it*.
question mark ?	The punctuation mark that should be used at the end of a question. An indirect question does not need one: 'Barbara asked if she could bring her sister to the party.'	'How many students are going to the party?' Barbara asked.
quotation mark ' ' or " "	Another name for inverted commas.	*'Can I bring my sister to the party?'* Barbara asked.
references	A list of all the works referred to in an essay, paper or book. See Chapter 13 and compare with *bibliography*.	The book referred to in the text was not cited in Gus's list of references.

Word	Definition and notes	Examples
referencing conventions	A set of conventions that governs how references should be laid out. These may conform to a known citation style, or may just be the 'house style' of a publisher or academic department.	Students are sometimes told: we do not mind which referencing conventions you follow as long as you are consistent. In such a case, they are advised to find a citation style they like.
relative pronoun	A pronoun that indicates a relationship with a noun or pronoun in another part of the sentence. It is used to introduce a subordinate (adjectival) clause. See especially Chapter 9. Note that the pronoun might introduce a restrictive clause (as in the first and third examples) or a descriptive clause (as in the second example).	This is the brother *who* invited his friend to the party. Eddie, *who* is Kim's brother, is studying law in Edinburgh. This is the ball *that* the dog found.
restrictive clause	A clause introduced by a relative pronoun that defines or restricts the noun (or equivalent) in the main clause.	Mark is the one *whom Barbara likes best*. Abel opened the file *that Gus had copied*.
run-on sentence	A sentence that should be separated from the previous one by a conjunction or appropriate punctuation (not a comma). Alternatively, the sentence could be turned into a phrase.	*Barbara has not done enough studying for her exam, this is because she spends too much time on learning grammar.* The above is a run-on sentence that would be better if it were shorter. 'This' (subject) and 'is' (verb) make the clause a main one. If these words are removed, then there is no run-on sentence.
scare quotes ' ' or " "	Inverted commas (quotation marks) used to indicate some doubt about a term or to suggest that this is not conventional usage. Use sparingly, if at all.	This is not what '*educated*' speakers do.
semicolon ;	A punctuation mark that separates. It is particularly used in complex lists to mark a longer pause than a comma. It is also sometimes used in place of a conjunction to avoid run-on sentences. See especially Chapters 7 and 10.	Kim has invited Mark to her party; *this* is because he rescued her.

'shall' or 'will'	Traditionally, it was considered correct to use 'shall' for the first person and 'will' for the second and third. The reverse was then for emphasis. This is made even more complicated by some dialect uses (e.g. Scots and Irish) that do it the other way round. (I shouldn't worry too much about this one!)	The old joke goes that a Scotsman or Irishman (depending on your prejudice) was seen in a loch or lough and heard to say: I *will* drown and no one *shall* save me. The pedantic people on the shore thought that he wanted to drown and left him to it.
[*sic*]	Latin for 'it is so', used to show that this was indeed what the author said, often to point out an error or assumption in that writing. See Chapter 13.	The student wrote: 'I done [*sic*] quite well in my essay.'
simile	A figure of speech in which one thing is likened to another, usually unexpectedly. It's compared with *metaphor* in Chapter 2.	Abel thinks that punctuation is *like the lines on a tennis court.*
split infinitive	It is considered by some people to be inappropriate to split the 'to' form of a verb, as in the *Star Trek* example '*To boldly go*'. Most grammar books suggest that this is pedantry, though it often sounds better if it is avoided.	The position of an adverb can have a major impact on meaning. It may even be appropriate to split an infinitive. I tried to write my essay correctly. I tried *to correctly write* my essay. I correctly tried to write my essay.
Standard English	The dialect of English that is regarded as educated. It is taught in schools and used in formal situations. Unlike other dialects, it is not exclusively associated with a region of the UK. See Chapter 3.	No one says this outwith Scotland. 'Outwith' is a Scottish word. The Standard English version would be: No one says this *outside* Scotland. (This may change; 'outwith' could possibly eventually be absorbed into Standard English.)
subject	The person, thing or idea that a sentence or clause is about. The agent for the verb. See Chapter 4. The subject of the sentence might be a phrase or even a clause.	In olden days, *teachers* were treated with great respect. *What Abel is doing* makes Barbara very worried.
subjunctive	The subjunctive form of a verb is used to express uncertainty or possibility. It is becoming rare, except for very specific phrases.	'Far *be* it from me to question your grammar,' Barbara said to Eddie, 'but if I *were* you, I'd check my relative clauses.'
subordinate clause	A clause that cannot function as a sentence by itself. See Chapters 6, 7 and 9. There are different types of subordinate clauses, relating to their function in a sentence: as a noun, an adjective or an adverb.	It is useful to know about subordinate clauses *because you might have too many of them*. The above is an adverbial clause – saying something about the verb in the main clause.
subordinating conjunction	A conjunction that introduces a subordinate clause.	*Although* Kim has been working hard, she still hasn't finished her dissertation.

Word	Definition and notes	Examples
summarize	Provide a miniature version of a piece of text, incorporating all the main points. It is a useful skill to avoid plagiarism. See Chapter 13 and compare with *paraphrase*.	The essay instruction asked students to 'summarize in your own words', which encouraged them to identify the writer's main points without plagiarizing them.
synonym	A word that means the same as another. This is not as common as people might think; there are many shades of meaning, so it often refers to very nearly the same meaning rather than exactly the same.	In some situations, 'dishevelled' would be a synonym for 'abandoned', but only when talking about hair or clothing.
syntax	Grammatical structure in sentences. Most of this book is about syntax.	The lecturer thought that the following sentences showed poor use of syntax: *The essay explores the relationship of power to status, it goes without saying that this is important. Being what is likely to give people power.*
tense	The form of a verb that indicates the time of the action.	Some books suggest that there are only two tenses: present (he *writes*) and past (he *wrote*). All other situations use auxiliary verbs.
text annotation	Adding comments to someone else's writing; a facility allowed by some word processing packages to comment on a document. This can be a useful facility for helping each other; some tutors are using this for assessment. See Chapter 14.	Abel had used the comment feature to make notes for the next draft of his essay. This was what finally exposed Gus's plagiarism.
thesaurus	A book that is systematically arranged so that it is easy to find synonyms or closely related words – and their opposite (antonyms). It is important to use the punctuation of the lists as guidance to find closely related words; if you don't understand a word, it may not be an idiomatic replacement.	Here is what Roget's Thesaurus (1962) says about the word *dictionary*: '*rhyming d., polyglot d.; lexicon, wordbook, wordstock, word-list, glossary, vocabulary; thesaurus, gradus; compilation, concordance.*'
topic sentence	The example shows this paragraph's topic sentence in italics.	*The topic sentence is the sentence in a paragraph that tells you what it is about.* The other sentences extend it or exemplify it. It frequently comes first in the paragraph but may come at the end.

transitive verb	A verb that takes an object. Some verbs are both transitive and intransitive; others, such as 'like' or 'bring', are always transitive. See Chapter 5 and *intransitive verb*. Some verbs that are in phrases are always transitive, e.g. 'wait for'. Unlike intransitive verbs, transitive ones can be made passive, though this gets awkward with phrases.	Barbara *likes* Abel. Barbara *looks forward to* the party.
Turnitin	A proprietary name for plagiarism software.	Turnitin has tools for staff and students to support good essay writing.
verb	The word denoting action in a sentence. There may be more than one verb, but there must be at least one and it should be finite (complete). See especially Chapter 5, but this word recurs throughout the book.	Abel *studies* science. Barbara *is* a Gemini. Kim *benefits from* her friends.
voice	A way of categorizing verbs to show their relationship with the subject: active or passive. You'll also see 'voice' being used to refer to who is allowed to be heard in the writing.	By using the *passive voice*, I can either hide the agent or draw attention to it. The soldier *was executed*. The soldier *was executed* by his own general. Students' own voices should be heard in their essays.
who or whom	Who is used as the subject of the verb; whom is used as the object.	Barbara called the shopowner *who* had threatened Kim. Barbara called the shopowner *whom* Kim had offended.

Bibliography

I consulted many books and several Internet sites to help me to write this book. Some of the following are referenced within the book, others are not. This is a list of my own recommendations, but there are many other excellent examples too.

Amis, K. (1997) *The King's English*. London: HarperCollins.
> Kingsley Amis was an excellent writer who had strong, often controversial, views. This book doesn't pull any punches, but does encourage us to steer an appropriate course between the sloppy and overly punctilious.

Burchfield, R. (ed.) (1996) *The New Fowler's Modern English Usage*, 3rd edn. Oxford: Clarendon.
> There are several editions of this classic reference book. There are debates about whether this edition preserves the ethos of Fowler's original work. It both records the changing uses of English and makes recommendations for 'correct' usage.

Burt, A. (2004) *Quick Solutions to Common Errors in English*. Oxford: How to Books.
> There are many mistakes in spelling, punctuation and grammar that students make repeatedly. Burt lists them alphabetically and offers useful tips on getting them right.

Chambers Dictionary (2003) Edinburgh: Chambers.
> Chambers is my favourite dictionary, but this is a personal choice and there are many other good ones. There are later editions.

Collinson, D., Kirkup, G., Kyd, R. and Slocombe, L. (1992) *Plain English*, 2nd edn. Buckingham: Open University Press.
> There are some useful quizzes and advice on typical problems in spelling, punctuation and grammar.

Cottrell, S. (2003) *Skills for Success*. London: Palgrave Macmillan.
> Stella Cottrell has written a number of study skills books. This one is subtitled 'The Personal Development Planning Handbook', and is very useful for anyone who is undertaking reflective writing for PDP.

Crystal, D. (1987) *The Cambridge Encyclopaedia of Language*. Cambridge: Cambridge University Press.
> This is the edition referenced in Chapter 7; a later one is available. It is a fascinating book, so it can be distracting.

Elbow, P. (1973) *Writing without Teachers*. Oxford: Oxford University Press.
> For Peter Elbow, fretting about grammar and rules about Standard English often gets in the way of just getting things written. He promotes the technique of freewriting – very useful for finding out what you are thinking about.

Fairclough, N. (1989) *Language and Power*. London: Longman
> This book got me thinking about the way language is used in institutions to 'position' people.

Gowers, E. (1973) (revised by Sir Bruce Fraser) *The Complete Plain Words*. London: HMSO.
This is a classic book for civil servants to encourage them to write clearly. It is itself well written and contains some lovely examples.

Kahn, J. (ed.) (1985) *The Right Word at the Right Time*. London: Readers Digest Association.
I bought this book in a second-hand bookshop a few years ago and have found it invaluable as a reference book and also a source of diverting articles – e.g. on 'English around the world'. I was interested to see that Palmer (2003) also references it.

Kipfer, B.A. (ed.) (2006) *Roget's New Millennium Thesaurus*, V 1.3.1. Lexico Publishing Group, LLC.
This is the most recent version of Roget's Thesaurus, though an older version was referred to in the Glossary. There is an associated website at http://thesaurus. reference.com/

Murray, R. (2006) *How to Write a Thesis*. Maidenhead: Open University Press.
If you are doing a PhD or other sustained piece of writing, this will help you to get through it. Rowena Murray emphasizes the process of writing, for example promoting freewriting as described by Elbow (1973).

Palmer, R. (2003) *The Good Grammar Guide*. London: Routledge.
This is a particularly helpful book for students, and I like Palmer's down-to-earth style.

Peck, J. and Coyle, M. (1999) *The Student's Guide to Writing*. London: Macmillan.
The authors present a very practical guide for students, containing useful summaries of key issues in grammar, punctuation and spelling.

Truss, L. (2003) *Eats, Shoots and Leaves*. London: Profile Books.
This is a book to read when you have become passionate about punctuation and want to preserve high standards. It's also very funny; but you do need to understand why the author is taking such a stance.

The following books provided examples for analysis.

Bloom, H. (1994) *The Western Canon*. London: Papermac.
Bryson, B. (2003) *A Short History of Nearly Everything*. London: Black Swan.
Dickens, C. (1837/1963) *The Pickwick Papers*. London: Collins.
Dreyfus, H. (2001) *On the Internet*. Abingdon: Routledge.
Kemp Smith, N. (translator) (1933) *Immanuel Kant's Critique of Pure Reason*. London: Macmillan.
Medawar, P. (1986) Lucky Jim. In *The Strange Case of the Spotted Mice and Other Classic Essays on Science*. Oxford: Oxford University Press.
Pirsig, R. (1974) *Zen and the Art of Motorcycle Maintenance*. Aylesbury: Corgi.
Popper, K. (1962) *The Open Society and its Enemies*, 5th edn. London: Routledge & Kegan Paul.
Silver, B. (1998) *The Ascent of Science*. Oxford: Oxford University Press.
Wright, P. (1994) *Introduction to Engineering*, 2nd edn. New York: John Wiley.

An example of one of many useful websites is the Online Writing Lab at Purdue University:

owl.english.purdue.edu/handouts/grammar/

Finally, the CD track 'Phonetic Punctuation' that Abel and Kim enjoyed so much can be heard on Victor Borge's *Phonetically Speaking – And Don't Forget the Piano!* Jasmine Records 2001.

Index

Related books from Open University Press
Purchase from www.openup.co.uk or order through your local bookseller

WRITING AT UNIVERSITY 3/E
A GUIDE FOR STUDENTS

Crème and Lea

Writing at University offers guidance on how to develop the writing you have to do at university along with a greater understanding of what is involved in this complex activity. Writing is seen as a tool for learning as well as a product to be assessed. The importance of what you yourself can bring as a writer to your academic writing is stressed throughout the book.

The book looks at an array of writing projects, including essays, reports and dissertations, and analyzes what is expected of each form of assignment. The authors provide examples of student writing and reflections on writing by both tutors and students.

This edition includes new sections on:

- Making an argument and persuading your reader
- Using sources creatively
- Avoiding plagiarism
- Writing online
- Further sources of information about academic writing

Writing at University is an essential resource for all college and university students, including postgraduates, who wish to develop their academic writing. It will also be an invaluable aid for tutors in supporting their students

Contents
Acknowledgments – You and university writing – Getting started – Writing for different courses – Beginning with the title – Reading as part of writing – Organizing and shaping your writing – Making an argument and persuading your reader – Making good use of your sources – Putting yourself into your academic writing – Putting it together – Completing the assignment and preparing for next time – Exploring different kinds of writing – Learning journals and reflective writing – Further reading and some additional sources – References – Index

2008   208pp
978–0–335–22116–5 (Paperback)